THE KENNEDYS
PORTRAIT OF A FAMILY

THE KENNEDYS
PORTRAIT OF A FAMILY

FIRST EDITION

First published in 2007 by:
Collins Design,
An Imprint of HarperCollins*Publishers*
10 East 53rd Street
New York, NY 10022
Tel: (212) 207-7000
Fax: (212) 207-7654
collinsdesign@harpercollins.com
www.harpercollins.com

Distributed throughout the world by:
HarperCollins*Publishers*
10 East 53rd Street
New York, NY 10022
Fax: (212) 207-7654

Design by Agnieszka Stachowicz and Christine Heslin

Library of Congress Cataloging-in-Publication Data
Avedon, Richard.
The Kennedys : portrait of a family / Richard Avedon;
Shannon Thomas Perich. -- 1st ed.
p. cm.
Includes bibliographical references.
ISBN-13: 978-0-06-113816-4 (hardcover)
ISBN-10: 0-06-113816-9 (hardcover)
1. Kennedy, John F. (John Fitzgerald), 1917-1963--Family--Pictorial works. 2. Kennedy, John F. (John Fitzgerald), 1917-1963--Pictorial works. 3. Onassis, Jacqueline Kennedy, 1929-1994--Pictorial works. 4. Kennedy, Caroline, 1957---Pictorial works. 5. Kennedy, John F. (John Fitzgerald), 1960-1999--Pictorial works. 6. Presidents--United States--Pictorial works. 7. Presidents--United States--Family--Pictorial works. 8. Kennedy family--Pictorial works. I. Perich, Shannon Thomas. II. Title. III. Title: John F. Kennedys.

E843.A94 2007
973.922092'2--dc22

2006037851

Printed in China
First Printing, 2007

RICHARD AVEDON
THE KENNEDYS
PORTRAIT OF A FAMILY

Shannon Thomas Perich | Foreword by Robert Dallek

COLLINS | DESIGN
An Imprint of HarperCollins*Publishers*

This book is dedicated to
the memory of my mother,
Susan Whitley Thomas,
and my own family,
Scott, Thomas, and Maeve

CONTENTS

ACKNOWLEDGMENTS

I owe many thanks to those who have offered support and shared their enthusiasm, expertise, and professional skills. They have all helped shape this book, and for that I am enormously grateful.

My colleagues at the National Museum of American History are invaluable personal and professional resources, especially my colleague in the Photographic History Collection, Michelle Delaney; my in-house editor, Joan Mentzer; and the head of Information Technology and Communications, David Allison. Additional thanks go to Joan Boudreau, Jim Gardner, and Susan Walther. Chris Cottrill and Stephanie Thomas in the National Museum of American History's library are a researcher's best friends. The bevy of interns who have aided with cataloging and research includes Rebecca Bower, Nicole Drinkard, Robyn Einhorn, and Kelly Johnson. Joy Weiner of the Smithsonian's Archives of American Art was gracious and enormously helpful.

The Collins Design staff members were excellent collaborators, and I share the success of this book with them: Elizabeth Viscott Sullivan, Marta Schooler, Ilana Anger, and Roni Alexrod. I'd also like to thank visionary book designers Agnieszka Stachowicz and Christine Heslin.

Caroline Kennedy Schlossberg and Tom McNaught of the Kennedy Library Foundation graciously allowed access to materials in Jacqueline Bouvier Kennedy Onassis' private papers. And no Kennedy book is complete without the assistance of archivists James B. Hill and Stephen Plotkin at the John F. Kennedy Library in Boston, Massachusetts.

Dodie Kazanjian and David M. Lubin independently provided useful feedback. Douglas Kirkland provided a vital photographer's view of *LOOK's* art department.

A special note of thanks goes to Norma Stevens and James Martin at The Richard Avedon Foundation for their openness and support of this project.

Avedon's photography was painstakingly reproduced by Smithsonian photographer Hugh Talman and finessed by David Sterling.

I am honored that renowned historian Robert Dallek graciously agreed to write the Foreword to the book.

Last, but not least, I'd like to thank my family and friends: Kathleen Thomas, Barbara and Steve Arnold, Sandy and Sonny Hale, Grandma Whitley, Jack and Carolyn Perich, Ray Thomas, Henry Horenstein, Paula Fleming, Leslie London, and Lauren Telchin-Katz. Thomas and Maeve, thank you for letting me work late and all those weekends. And Scott, for your unfailing belief in me and smart critique, thank you.

FOREWORD

In 1901, William McKinley, a popular second-term president, was assassinated in Buffalo, New York. In 1944, 43 years after his death, he had joined the ranks of other largely nameless, faceless presidents like the two Harrisons, William Henry and Benjamin, Millard Fillmore, Rutherford B. Hayes, James A. Garfield, and Chester Arthur. McKinley's wife and family were as obscure as most retired or defeated members of Congress.

Forty-three years after John F. Kennedy's abbreviated presidency at the hands of an assassin, JFK, Jacqueline, and the children, Caroline and John Jr., remain as vital a part of the national political scene as if the Kennedys were still in the White House. Unlike McKinley, who Theodore Roosevelt, Woodrow Wilson, and Franklin D. Roosevelt so greatly eclipsed, Kennedy has not had to stand in the shadow of Lyndon B. Johnson, Richard M. Nixon, Gerald Ford, Jimmy Carter, George H.W. Bush, Bill Clinton, or George W. Bush, all of whom left (or in George W.'s case will leave) the White House under one cloud or another. Only Ronald Reagan seems to vie with Kennedy for the public's continuing affection, but no one in the Reagan family can match the star quality of the Kennedy clan.

Kennedy's appeal, however, rests on more than the flawed records of his successors. It's not as if Kennedy's presidential performance was without its own failings: the disastrous invasion of Cuba at the Bay of Pigs in April 1961; the unsuccessful meeting with Nikita Khrushchev in Vienna in June 1961; the failed efforts to topple Castro's government that helped provoke the Cuban Missile Crisis in October 1962; and the expansion of America's military involvement in Vietnam between 1961 and 1963, which some have described as the prelude to Lyndon Johnson's ruinous war that ultimately resulted in more than 58,000 U.S. military deaths, have not been sources of Kennedy's high standing with so many Americans for over four decades.

The enduring attraction to Kennedy has much more to do with his inspirational qualities. Presidents seem to be remembered less for their domestic and foreign policy accomplishments—unless there were extraordinary far-reaching actions such as FDR's social security law, LBJ's civil and voting rights measures, or such decisive military victories as Lincoln's defeat of secession in the Civil War and FDR's triumph over Nazism, fascism, and Japanese militarism in World War II—than their famous pronouncements. Washington's Farewell Address, Monroe's Doctrine, Woodrow Wilson's Fourteen Points, FDR's "nothing to fear but fear itself," Eisenhower's warning about the military-industrial complex, and LBJ's invocation of a Great Society are cases in point.

Kennedy gave the country more than one memorable phrase: most famously "Ask not what your country can do for you. Ask what you can do for your country"; and the still resonant "Mankind must do away with war or war will do away with mankind."

Yet ultimately, in this age when visual images seem to make a greater impression than words on people all over the world, it is the abundant and easily accessible television tapes and photographs of Kennedy and his family that continue to excite attraction to and affection for what can fairly be described as America's first family.

Kennedy was our first television president. His memorable first TV debate with Richard Nixon during the 1960 presidential campaign has been a model of how to reach undecided voters, though no candidate since Kennedy has been as successful in using such a moment to gain a significant advantage in a close election. People who heard the Kennedy–Nixon debate on their radios thought that Nixon had won, but the much larger viewing audience saw Kennedy as the winner. It was not just Kennedy's appearance but the contrast with Nixon's that served JFK so well. Nixon, dressed in a light gray suit, "faded into a fuzzed outline," one observer said, "while Kennedy in his dark suit had the crisp picture edge of contrast." A pale, thin Nixon showed the aftermath of a hospitalization from a knee infection. Mayor Richard Daley of Chicago, speaking of Nixon, quipped, "My God! They've embalmed him before he even died."

Fewer things served Kennedy so well during and since his presidency as his use of live televised news conferences. Those meetings with the press were unprecedented and considered risky—a verbal slip or awkward body language before the cameras could prove to be a serious political disadvantage. But Kennedy understood that television was a great benefit to him in promoting support for his domestic and foreign policies. His youthful appearance combined with his evident charm, wit, and ability to articulate his policies converted many in the press and millions of citizens into Kennedy admirers and supporters. The news conference, a regular feature of his administration, educated Americans and inspired confidence that he was providing effective leadership during some of the most difficult moments of the cold war.

The photographs in this book are first of all a tribute to the artistry of Richard Avedon, America's greatest twentieth-century photographer. As Adam Gopnik said in *The New Yorker's* October 2004 tribute to Avedon and his genius, "To know Dick Avedon was to know the sun. He radiated out daily and early on a circle of friends, family and colleagues, who drew on his light and warmth for sustenance.... As long as people remain curious about life in the twentieth century, they will turn to Avedon's photographs to see how it looked and what it meant."

As long as interest about JFK, Jackie, and the children exists, people will turn to Avedon's "Observations of the 35th First Family." The introduction to this book says it best, "Avedon's photographs of John and Jacqueline Kennedy and their two children combine politics, style, public interest, and photographic history to provide a glimpse of historical figures who have deeply touched American life." Avedon took these portraits of Jack and Jacqueline, husband and wife, father and daughter, mother and daughter, mother and newborn son, Caroline and John Jr. in early January 1961 before the presidential inauguration. To a large degree, from Kennedy's perspective, they were an exercise in expanding and solidifying his hold on the public. Having won the election by the narrowest of margins and being the youngest man ever elected to the highest American office with the youngest first lady in the country's history, Kennedy was mindful of the need to build national and international confidence in his capacity to govern.

Richard Avedon's photographs humanized Kennedy and his family and encouraged the view that here was a man and a woman who were America at its best and were born to govern. Long before the myth of Camelot took hold in the aftermath of the president's assassination, Kennedy had established himself and his family as the country's democratic royalty: a man and a family who inspired a renewed belief in America's capacity to withstand the domestic (an abrasive racial divide) and foreign (Communism's challenge) threats to the country's future. More than 40 years later, with new national divisions and external dangers undermining hopes for better days, people will turn once again to Avedon's photographs and memories of the Kennedys with a renewed belief in the promise of American life.

—Robert Dallek, December 2006

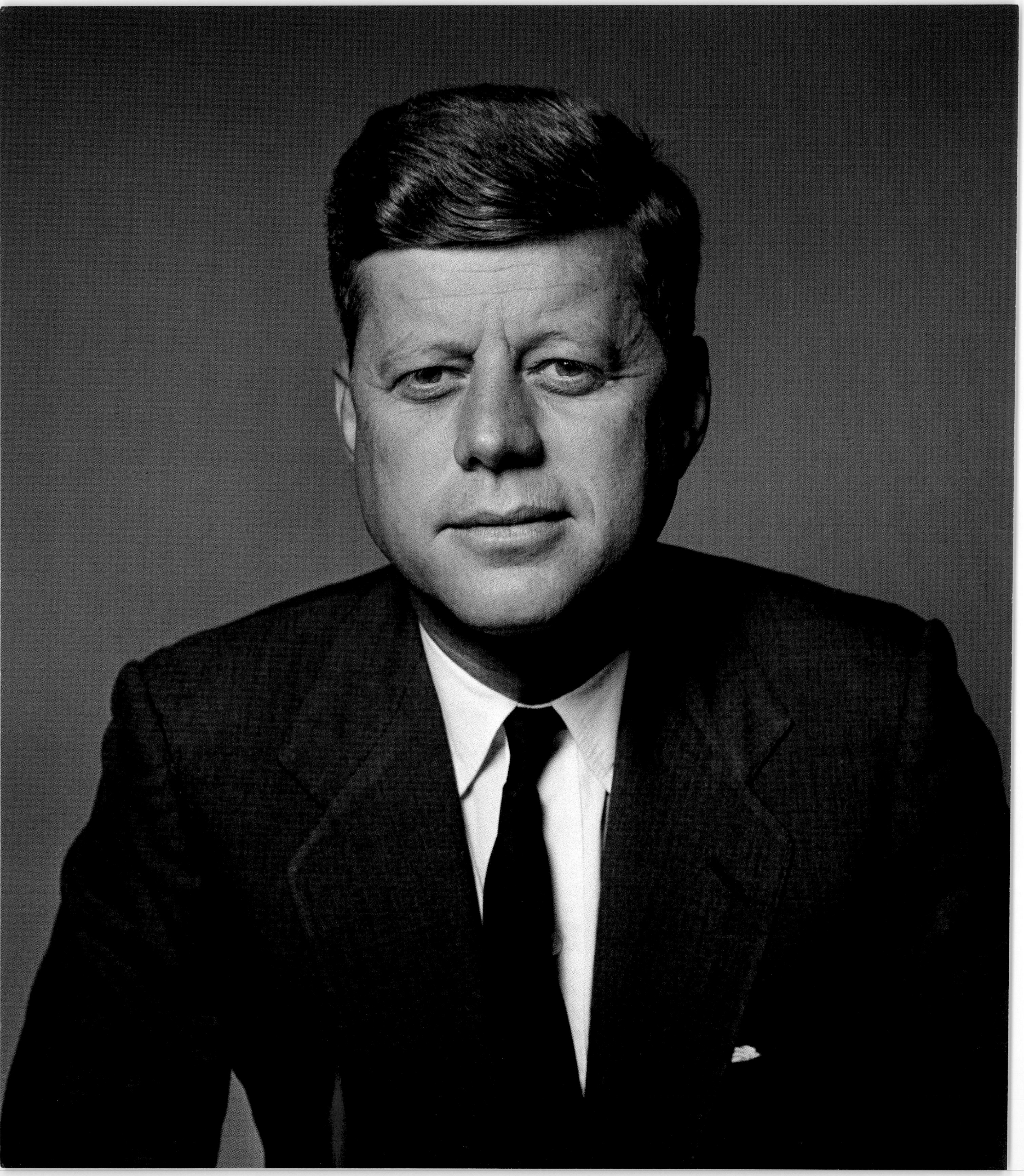

All this will not be finished in the first 100 days.

Nor will it be finished in the first 1,000 days,

nor in the life of this Administration,

nor even perhaps in our lifetime on this planet.

BUT LET US BEGIN.

—John F. Kennedy, Inaugural Address, January 20, 1961

INTRODUCTION

On January 3, 1961, the weather was a breezy and comfortable 75 degrees along the stretch of beach at the Kennedy compound in Palm Beach, Florida.

Inside the rambling Mediterranean-style house at 1095 North Ocean Boulevard, Richard Avedon was setting up his portable portrait studio in the drafty living room, while Mr. Kenneth of New York styled Jacqueline Kennedy's hair, Rose Kennedy fretted over Caroline and John Jr.'s clothes, and aides took memos and relayed phone messages to president-elect John F. Kennedy.

Avedon, now at the height of his profession, had come to Palm Beach to create photo exclusives for *Harper's Bazaar* and *LOOK* magazines. *The Kennedys: Portrait of a Family* presents this unique set of images from the Smithsonian's collection and revisits the only known formal pre-inaugural photographs of the president-elect and his family to examine a fascinating intersection of photography, fashion, and history.

In January 1961, women still wore gloves as part of their daily attire and men regularly used dressing like Brylcreem™ in their hair. "The Twist," Chubby Checker's song and dance, was all the rage. The Berlin Wall did not yet exist. The Beatles and the Rolling Stones had not yet invaded America. Nearly a year earlier, the Greensboro Four had staged a sit-in at an all-white Woolworth's lunch counter in North Carolina, sparking a wave of similar sit-ins across the South. The Soviet missile that had shot down an American U-2 spy plane the previous spring had exacerbated the tension between the United States and Soviet Union. Television was barely twenty years old. Picture magazines like *LOOK* and *Life* were an important mainstream source of information and entertainment, and fashion magazines like *Vogue* and *Harper's Bazaar* were the most imaginative and technically advanced users of photography.

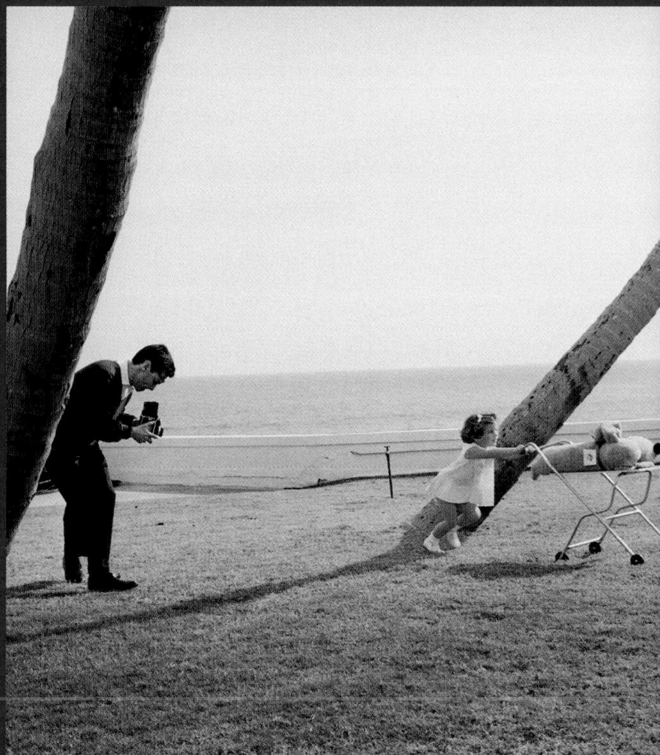

Richard Avedon photographing Caroline Kennedy for the February 28, 1961, *LOOK* photo spread. This image was the last on the roll of film used for the *Harper's Bazaar* photo session. For the full contact sheet, see page 89.

Avedon's photographs of the Kennedys for the February 28 issue of *LOOK* take their place among the many lively, energetic family pictures by the great Kennedy chroniclers. Stanley Tretick, Jacques Lowe, and Mark Shaw each had a unique perspective, creating culturally significant images within the photographic parameters established by the Kennedys. The photographs for the February 1961 issue of *Harper's Bazaar*, however, are starkly different—they were created within Avedon's parameters.

Richard Avedon was as much a leader in the development of American visual culture as he was a participant in it. He worked mostly for *Harper's Bazaar*, but also photographed for *LOOK*, *Life*, and a variety of advertising clients. In 1957, he was the creative consultant for Stanley Donen's movie *Funny Face*, which starred Audrey Hepburn and Fred Astaire. Astaire's character, Dick Avery, was modeled after Richard (Dick) Avedon, and many characters in the movie were based on his colleagues and editors at *Harper's Bazaar*. In 1958, *Popular Photography* named him one of the ten greatest photographers in the world.

Like Avedon, the Kennedys were leaders of and participants in American visual culture. In the 1920s, John F. Kennedy's father, Joseph Kennedy Sr., bought and sold Hollywood studios, produced films, and owned movie theaters. Much of the elder Kennedy's knowledge about the power of the visual image was effectively applied to his son's political career: many journalists and historians cite Kennedy's compelling performance during the first of the televised presidential campaign debates with Richard Nixon as a deciding factor of his electoral win. Joe Kennedy's close relationship with Henry Luce, editor in chief and principal stockholder of Time, Inc., kept John's and later Jackie's faces on the covers of *Time* and *Life*.

When Richard Avedon made these images between the presidential election and the inauguration, the Kennedys were well known through pictures and television and had established a style in which they preferred to be photographed. Jackie's importance as a fashion trendsetter was just beginning to take hold, and the *Harper's Bazaar* sitting provided a new arena in which the Kennedys could present themselves.

The Smithsonian Institution retains the *Harper's Bazaar* photographs as part of a larger donation by Avedon and objects donated by the Kennedys. The Smithsonian also holds many more items that relate to and place these two American icons in historical context. Richard Avedon had a long relationship with the Smithsonian, beginning in 1962 with his first one-man photography exhibition. The exhibition was held at the Institution's Arts and Industries Building, and Avedon donated all of the exhibit's images. Through his gifts over the years, he created a rich record of both American and photographic history. With the exception of his *In the American West* and *Democracy* projects, the Institution holds representations of a wide range of Avedon's work, from his early pivotal image *Italy #9*, Noto, Sicily, September 5, 1947, that brought him to the attention of *Harper's Bazaar* art director Alexey Brodovitch to his contributions for events related to September 11, 2001.

Avedon captured the essence of important mid-twentieth-century writers and thinkers, stage and film performers, musicians, politicians, and activists through his portraits. His advertising work improved the sales of clothing and various other products. Those advertisements were published in many popular magazines, like *Life*, *Vogue*, and *Rolling Stone*, as well as in specialized journals, such as *Graphis*. He was among the highest-paid and sought-after photographers, and his clients included Pabst, DuPont, Cartier, and Douglas Aircraft. Avedon was instrumental in the success of Revlon's 1952 "Fire and Ice" ad campaign, which featured his photograph of Dorian Leigh, a platinum streak in her hair, wearing a silver sequined dress with a bright red cape. The two-page spread also featured an edgy but humorous questionnaire to determine if the female reader was "made for fire and ice." Avedon was also one of several famous photographers who participated in Maidenform's "I Dreamed" campaign. One of his images features a woman in a silver lamé bra; the photograph and the bra are part of the Smithsonian's collections.

Avedon's participation in creating visual culture through advertisements continued throughout his career. Those memorable and sometimes spoofed 1980s' television ads for Calvin Klein's perfume "Obsession" were directed by Avedon. In the November 1, 2004, issue of *The New Yorker* that featured Avedon's last photographic project, *Democracy*, Hermès, Harry Winston, and Kenneth Cole ran advertisements created with Avedon's images.

Many of the Kennedy–related materials—campaign literature and buttons, event programs, and more—at the Smithsonian have been acquired through individuals other than the subjects. But Jackie Kennedy did follow

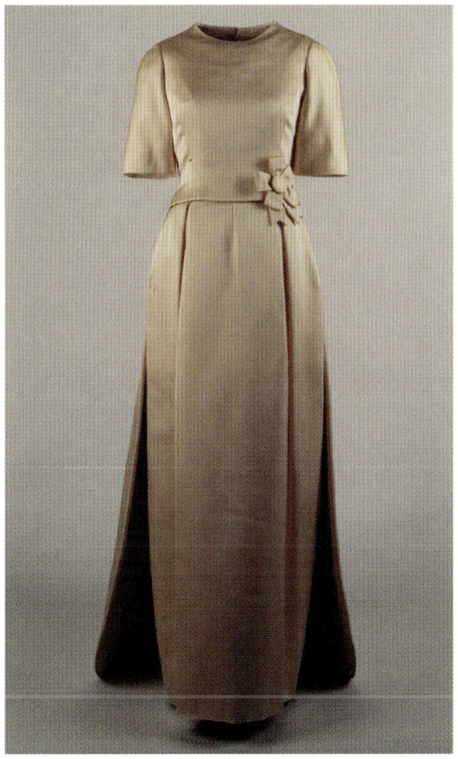

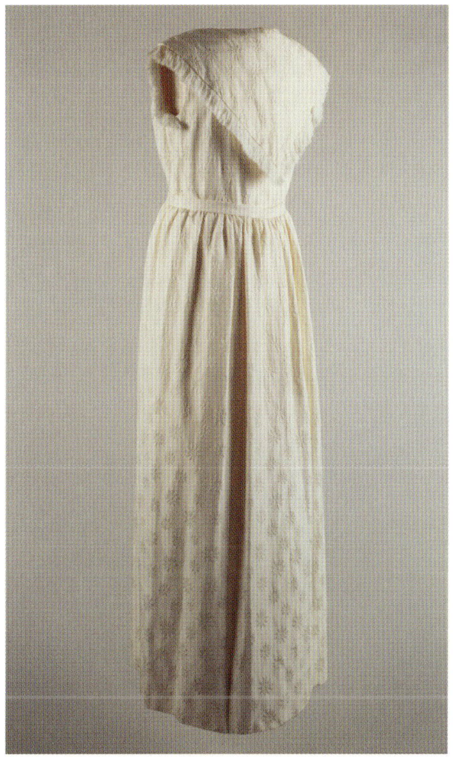

Far left: Jackie collaborated with Oleg Cassini to design the dress she wore to the January 19, 1961, pre-inaugural ball. She wore white as she considered it to be the "most ceremonial color." The cockade—a fabric rosette originally worn on the battlefield as a badge of loyalty—placed on her hip was a nod to her French heritage and love of history. **Left:** This daisy-embroidered ivory silk Hubert de Givenchy hostess gown recalls the style of dress in the 1780s.

the tradition of first ladies by donating her inaugural gown to the Smithsonian as well as the dress she purchased from Bergdorf Goodman for the inauguration. Rose Kennedy also donated the gown she wore to the inaugural ball; this was the same dress she had worn some twenty years earlier when she and Joseph Kennedy Sr., then the United States ambassador to Britain, were presented to King George VI and Queen Elizabeth.

Objects exhibited at the Smithsonian often require that we look back through history. Today the experience of seeing Avedon's photographs of the Kennedys is laden with dramatic irony, for we know how the story ends for three of the four sitters. Most people who were at least five years old on November 22, 1963, remember where they were and what they were doing when they learned President Kennedy was assassinated. Many more watched how Jackie handled herself and moved on with her life until her death on May 19, 1994. Still more can recall how John F. Kennedy Jr., his young wife, and her sister perished in a tragic airplane accident on July 16, 1999. As readers, we can't help but bring our personal experiences when we look at these photographs.

The 1960 presidential election was won by a very narrow margin. When Avedon photographed the Kennedys between the election and the inauguration, the time represented the height of hopeful anticipation for those who believed in John F. Kennedy, and the height of anxiety for those who did not. Avedon's photographs of John and Jacqueline Kennedy and their two children combine politics, style, public interest, and photographic history to provide a glimpse of historical figures who have deeply touched American life.

HARPER'S BAZAAR

Richard Avedon's photographs of John F. Kennedy, Jacqueline, three-year-old Caroline, and six-week-old John Jr. taken on January 3, 1961, appeared in the February issue of *Harper's Bazaar* as well as the February 28 issue of *LOOK* magazine.

In mid-February, through the Associated Press and other photo news services, the White House released twenty-one of these images, which allowed newspapers across the country to print a selection. Avedon's photographs from that single day of photography satisfied many agendas. Both magazines published portfolios. It was a prestigious sitting for Avedon. The Kennedys were able to satisfy public curiosity by publishing these images in widely read publications.

Although Kennedy was holding press conferences during this time, he and the photographers who traveled with him on the campaign trail were taking a break from one another. After the 1960 presidential election, photographs of Kennedy and his family continued to generate great interest, and John Jr.'s premature birth by cesarean section on November 25, 1960, only added to the public's curiosity. But with Jackie recovering from surgery and preparing to become first lady, and Kennedy establishing his cabinet, writing his inauguration speech, and traveling between Palm Beach, Washington, D.C., and New York, bringing the young family together long enough for a photo session was nearly impossible. By happy circumstances, Richard Avedon was permitted to photograph the president-elect and his family.

Surprisingly, very little is actually known about the details of the photo session. No one knows who coordinated and arranged the assignments from *Harper's Bazaar* and *LOOK*, and even the date of the session is in some question. Hearst Corporation, the owner of *Harper's Bazaar*, does not retain an archive. *LOOK* went out of business in 1971, and while the Library of Congress has some of its materials, it has no correspondence. The daily schedules kept by Jackie for herself and by Evelyn Lincoln for Kennedy are sketchy at best during this time. What really happened and how is only known by those present that day. Fortunately, various authors and diarists have recorded details, and archivists have preserved other elements that helped construct the story.

One of the most informative sources is a one-page article that ran in the February 6, 1961, issue of *Newsweek*. The unidentified author spoke with Avedon briefly about the photo sitting. In that same article, *Harper's Bazaar* editor Nancy White explains the origin of the sitting. "We approached Mrs. Kennedy. A number of people on staff know her personally, and it was such an obvious idea for our magazine since she's so fashionable." The article only mentions the *Harper's Bazaar* photographs, although we know that a second sitting that day produced the images for *LOOK*. White says it was Jackie they were interested in, as does Rose Fitzgerald Kennedy's 1974 autobiography, *Times to Remember*. While the arrangements might have been made to photograph Jackie, according to Avedon's daybook, Avedon's own intentions were to photograph "President-elect John Kennedy and family."

Perhaps getting Jackie to agree to be photographed would at least give Avedon proximity to the president-elect, and he would be able to entice Kennedy to sit for a few frames, especially for a mass-media publication like *LOOK*. It is not an unlikely scenario. Orlando Suero, who was on assignment for *McCall's* to photograph a "woman's interest" story on Jackie as a new wife in 1954 recalled, "John Kennedy kept sneaking himself into the pictures."

Jackie had appeared previously in *Harper's Bazaar*. In 1947, the year she was voted Debutante of the Year, Avedon photographed the fresh-faced Jacqueline Bouvier for an article on winter holiday dresses. In 1958, she was one of the magazine's "Six Faces of Beauty (see page 97)." Mrs. Patrick Guinness, Mrs. William S. Paley, and Mrs. Henry B. Middleton were sketched by Italian artist Lucian Guarnieri, while Avedon photographed Jackie, Mrs. Henry Fonda, and Princess Laudomia Hercolani of Italy. In the summer of 1960, *Harper's Bazaar* ran an article on the presidential candidates' wives, and Eve Arnold of Magnum photographed Jackie and Caroline at their Georgetown home.

Certainly Jackie knew the important photographers of the time and how their work was used by the media. The Kennedys employed and grew friendly with several photographers who documented their family and political activities. One photographer was Jacques Lowe, who began taking pictures of Kennedy's senatorial campaign in 1957. His photographs of Kennedy were used for everything from newspaper illustrations to campaign buttons. (Forty thousand of his Kennedy negatives were among the losses in the collapse of the World Trade Center towers on September 11, 2001.) Lowe published an article and photographs of the first-lady-to-be in the *Los Angeles Times* on January 8, 1961. He wrote, "Yet, one of the pleasures for me of working with her is that she appreciates photography as a creative medium, as opposed to some people in public life who consider photography a necessary nuisance."

Jackie's understanding of the functions of photography derived from her experiences on both sides of the lens. In 1951, at age twenty-two and just finishing college at George Washington University, she entered *Vogue's*

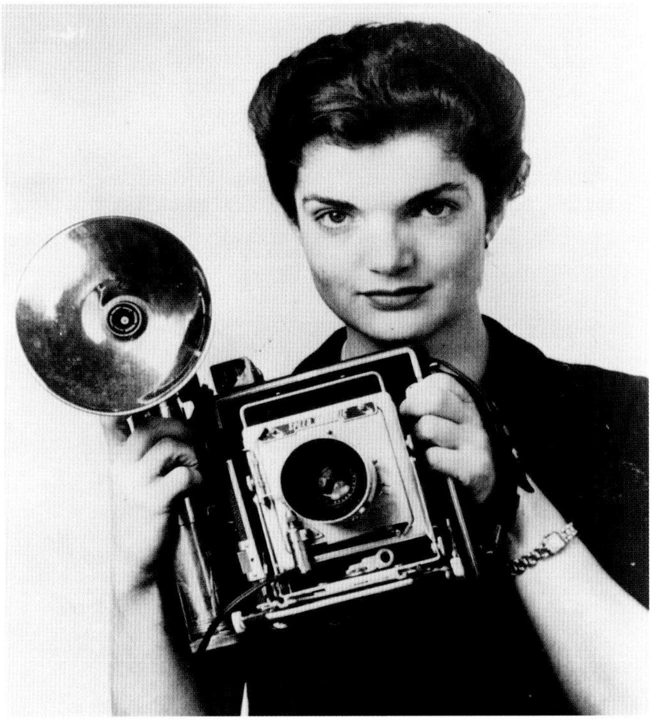

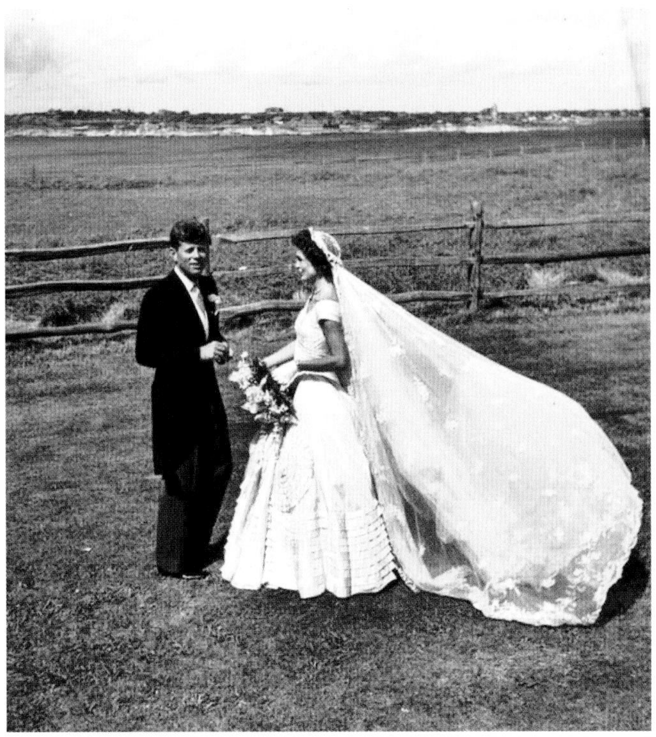

Top: Jackie during her tenure as the "Inquiring Camera Girl" at the *Washington Times-Herald* (now the *Washington Post*). She resigned from her position in 1953 and married John F. Kennedy in September of that year (**bottom**).

Prix de Paris writing contest. She won, but her mother thought the contest undignified and forced her to turn down the prize. But because she showed promise as a journalist, her stepfather Hugh Auchincloss helped to arrange a meeting with the editor of the *Washington Times-Herald*, Frank Waldrop. Waldrop reluctantly hired her as the "Inquiring Camera Girl," a post she held from 1952 to 1953. Waldrop remembers her fondly: "She didn't know one end of a camera from the other when she came to us. The other photographers pitched in to teach her. She was smart. She learned fast. She had real talent as an artist and a writer."

During her time at the paper, she contributed sketches, interviews, and photographs, beginning with Eisenhower's inauguration parade. She interviewed then Vice President Nixon and then Senator Kennedy about the Capitol Hill pages in her April 21, 1953, column, an article in which her future husband joked about switching jobs with a page who looked older than he did so the Capitol Police would stop thinking he was a tourist. Three weeks after Jackie resigned from her job, her picture appeared in the newspaper under the headline "Inquiring Camera Girl to be Sen. Kennedy's Bride." She returned to newspaper writing at the end of Kennedy's presidential campaign, penning a syndicated weekly column, "The Candidate's Wife," issued by the Democratic National Committee.

Public interest in Jackie and her fashion sensibilities heightened throughout Kennedy's presidential campaign. She was fully aware that photographs of her were not only meant to capture her as an individual and mother, but as a future first lady. In July 1960, William Moore wrote in the *Chicago Tribune*, "They [women] want to see what she is wearing, of course, and they want to see as much of the fabulous Kennedys as they can. But they also want to know if she really has the grace and poise of which they have heard, as well as the simple friendliness."

In his article for the *Los Angeles Times*, Jacques Lowe tried to satisfy Moore's questions and defend Jackie:

> *And over these years I have come to respect the relatively frail, beautiful and very intelligent Jacqueline Bouvier Kennedy. Much has been said by now about Mrs. Kennedy, and much of what has been said is wrong. Her great poise and tremendous dignity have been called cold, and her very real need for some privacy has been interpreted as shyness. I have always found her to be a private person with a great sense of herself, without conceit, a person who knows what she wants, what she likes and who she is. She has always shown real thoughtfulness and kindness toward people from all walks of life, and because she does know her own mind and isn't afraid of it, she has shown much independence and individuality of dress and manners. A delightful conversationalist, interested in everything and everyone, she is a joy to be with.*

The public craving to know Jackie did not subside, nor did her reluctance to give in to it. Throughout the campaign—and until her death—she sharply limited photography of herself and her children, unless she believed acceding to it was a means to an end. It would seem highly likely then that permitting Avedon to photograph her and her family for *Harper's Bazaar* was Jackie's choice.

An avid reader of fashion magazines for many years, Jackie was aware of how Avedon portrayed women. *The New Yorker's* Winthrop Sargeant described Avedon's approach in a profile of his work in 1958:

> *Avedon was widely conceded to have reached a previously unattained artistic level in fashion photography. A good deal of this accomplishment can be attributed to his imagination and resourcefulness in handling a camera, but some of it undoubtedly stems from the fact that his primary interest is not in fashion, but in women. In fashion photography, the human beings are, of course, beautiful women, as seen through his camera lens they actually do take on the semblance of leading ladies on the stage. They may, in passing, also make the clothes they are wearing seem desirable, but what principally attracts the eye is the spirited way they seem to be participating in psychological drama.*

Perhaps it seemed to Jackie that Avedon would portray her as something other than just a first lady in a beautiful dress—that his work might suggest her intellectual and emotional depth as well.

In Avedon's photographs, Jackie is clearly an easy and willing participant. It is also evident that Kennedy does not share her commitment to the sitting. In nearly all of the photographs with Jackie and John Jr., Kennedy seems stiff, distant, and restrained. He stands somewhat too far back and aside from Jackie to create a visually comfortable relationship between them. With his hands in his pockets, he appears to regard John Jr. with trepidation. In the photographs of Kennedy and Jackie together, he sits still, almost in the same pose from frame to frame, while Jackie seems to shift her position a bit, as if trying to chat and laugh with her husband and pose for Avedon simultaneously. Avedon graciously explained in the *Newsweek* article that "in a very charming way he was ill at ease.... Jacqueline said he

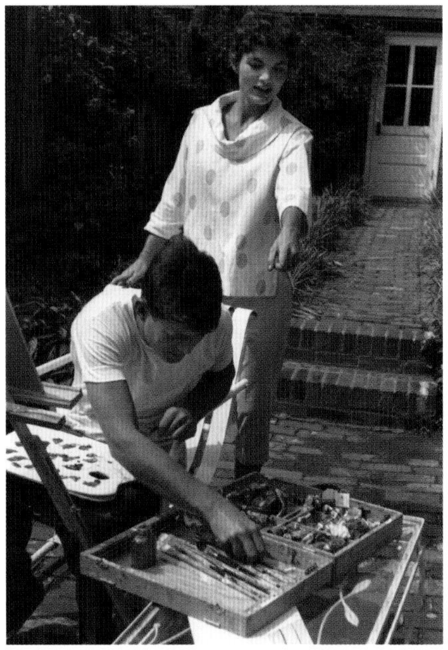

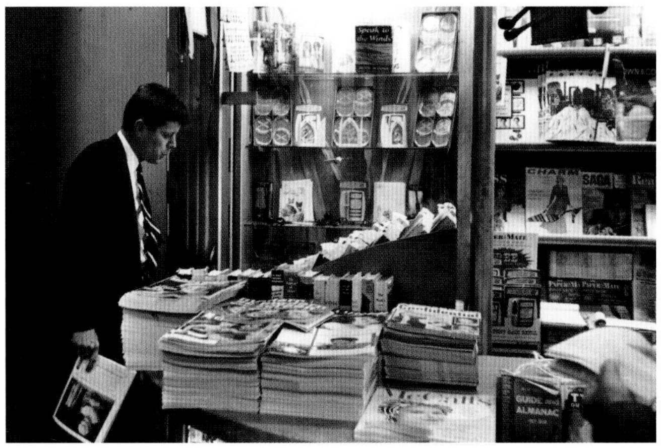

Top: Jackie gives Kennedy a painting lesson during one of many photo sessions for a story on her that appeared in *McCall's* in October 1954. Orlando Suero took this photograph on May 9, 1954. **Bottom:** John F. Kennedy, photographed by Verner Reed for *Life*, at a Boston, Massachusetts, newsstand in 1957.

always looks his best when he's talking to a crowd, and freezes up when he has his portrait taken." But Kennedy did have higher priorities than a sitting: that day he had been informed by the Eisenhower administration that the United States had severed diplomatic ties with Cuba. As Avedon said, "When I took Caroline's picture with her father, he was dictating memos to his secretary.... When I'd ask him to look around, he'd stop dictating. But the moment I finished, he'd start in where he left off. I've never seen such a display of mental control in my life."

In the photographs with Caroline, Kennedy is more engaged, relaxed, affectionate, and playful. As Avedon recalled for *Newsweek*, "When I wanted President Kennedy to play with Caroline, she stood on his lap while he held her by the knees and she leaned way forward and he would say, 'Let's pretend you're diving into the sea.'" By the end of the *Harper's Bazaar* photo session, Avedon had captured many touching moments between father and daughter, brother and sister, and mother and son. He also had successfully photographed the elegant and intriguing first-lady-to-be. Avedon, though, was his own harshest critic. He said, "I wanted to get a victory picture of Kennedy showing his big smile... But in no way did I get their real spirit of vitality. I was so impressed by the moment—it was one of the biggest assignments of my life—I just didn't make it."

Most people would hardly judge the photo sitting a failure. But like Avedon, Kennedy felt something was lacking. Rose Kennedy reported overhearing him say to LeMoyne Billings, a lifelong friend, "Well, that was certainly a morning wasted." It's likely that Avedon had anticipated this sort of response by Kennedy to a sitting for a fashion magazine and had previously arranged for

LOOK to acquire photographs more in line with the sort of outdoor, active photographs Kennedy preferred. Kennedy did not have a high regard for fashion magazines, and teased Jackie about them. His taste was pragmatic; he was less interested in artistic endeavors, favoring newspapers, news magazines, and history books. But he did understand the public's interest in photographs of the family and the political power of photography. In the preface to his biography, *An Unfinished Life: John F. Kennedy, 1917–1963*, Robert Dallek wrote, "As with all our most interesting public figures, Kennedy is an elusive character, a man who, like all politicians, worked hard to emphasize his favorable attributes and hide his limitations. He and those closest to him were extraordinarily skillful at creating positive images that continue to shape public impressions." Many of those "positive images" were made by photographers and publishers who perpetually promoted Kennedy's wholesome and youthful appearance.

Outdoor action shots of the Kennedys often appeared on the cover of *Life*. Avedon, who photographed Elizabeth Taylor, Audrey Hepburn, and other celebrities for *LOOK* and *Life*, was familiar with capturing images that would satisfy the photo editor, celebrities' images of themselves, and the reader's curiosity. His photographs for *LOOK* complied with the expectation and comfort level for Kennedy imagery. The *Harper's Bazaar* photographs stand respectfully against those in *LOOK* to represent Avedon's ideas about photography and fashion at that particular moment in time.

On January 3, 1961, Avedon arrived at the Kennedy compound with two assistants and his equipment, which included several cameras, lights, and the big roll of white paper he used to create stark backgrounds. In addition to hair stylist Mr. Kenneth, a dress fitter from Oleg Cassini was on hand. (Jackie's dresses weren't quite finished so she could only wear them for the duration of a few photographic frames.) Also present were John Jr.'s nurse, British nanny Maude Shaw; Jackie's secretary, Pamela Turnure; Kennedy's secretary, Evelyn Lincoln; several Secret Service agents; and numerous Kennedy friends and family members. Lincoln described the time as "... an exciting, fast-paced ride on a merry-go-round." In both the *Harper's Bazaar* and the *LOOK* contact sheets, various individuals can be seen at the edges of the images or even centered in the frames themselves. The resulting photographs speak highly to the focused collaboration between the sitters and the photographer to concentrate in what had to have been a chaotic environment.

Avedon's ability to connect with his subjects can be seen in the photographs of Jackie wearing the white pre-inaugural ball dress (see pages 99–107). She stays focused, only interrupted for three frames by Caroline. Avedon is likely suggesting the subtle changes in the way she holds her head. Jackie looks directly at the camera, holding the viewer's gaze with quiet intensity and elegantly asserting her control, strength, confidence, and beauty with a slightly defiant air. Avedon's intense, if only momentary, relationship with a sitter was sustained by the photographer during the printing process and conveyed through the layout.

Laura Wilson, writing many years later about her experience traveling with Avedon during his photo essay for *In the American West*, describes this connection well. "The speed and tension Avedon brought to a session transferred to the subject, concentrating the energy and compressing the space between them. This shared territory of intimacy allowed Avedon to see the slightest

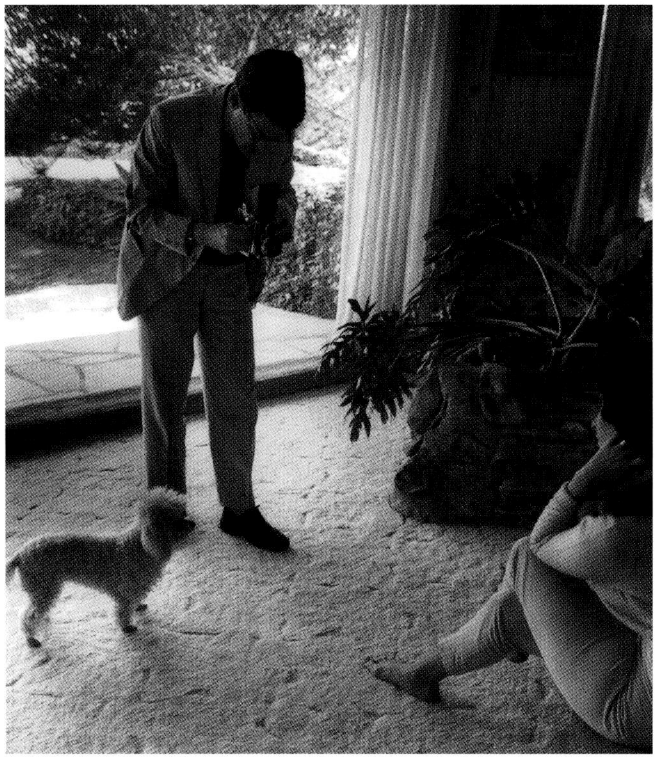

Robert Vose recorded Richard Avedon photographing Elizabeth Taylor in April 1956 for *LOOK*.

change of expression, to sense any shift of mood, to whisper encouragement and direction to his subject."

The set of photographs for "Avedon: Observations of the 34th First Family" (the typo was made by *Harper's Bazaar*; "34th" should have been "35th") is "the first in a monthly series of *Observations* by Richard Avedon on aspects of contemporary life," as the magazine stated. The *Observations* series came about as a result of a long working relationship with *Harper's Bazaar*'s esteemed art director Alexey Brodovitch and legendary editor Carmel Snow. The tightly cropped photos, the large amount of white space and minimal text, and the order of the images reflect Brodovitch's influence. (Brodovitch also designed Avedon's collaborative book with Truman Capote, *Observations*, published in 1959. Although there are many stylistic similarities between the book and the series, they were separate projects.)

It was well known that Oleg Cassini designed Jackie's dresses, but there is no mention of him. This omission would indicate that Avedon's photographs of the Kennedys were not intended as a fashion layout. The willingness to let photography stand on its own in the magazine was originally Snow's, although Nancy White was the magazine's editor at the time of the Kennedy sitting. The magazine reserved space in each issue for Avedon's nonfashion photography and the *Observations* series, and allowed him an extraordinary amount of control over his work.

The *Observations* series presented a variety of topics that held Avedon's interests. The Kennedys were his first subject—why remains unclear. Avedon was a creative photographer who worked closely with art directors and magazine editors. Whether he had full control of the content or suggestions were made by the editors is also unknown.

Over the course of 1961 Avedon created nine diverse photo essays, photographing members of the United Nations; teen pop idols like Conway Twitty and the Everly Brothers; the corpses of the Capuchin Catacombs in Palermo, Italy; babies from the New York Foundling Hospital; civil weddings at New York City Hall; weavers and ribbon makers; pets and their owners; and women in traditionally male careers, including doctors and a Korean university president.

In terms of timing, it is extraordinary that the photographs appeared in the February issue. The typo in the title indicates how rapidly the project was executed, particularly as magazines work a few months in advance of their publication date. In the case of the Kennedy images, perhaps two weeks passed from the Palm Beach sitting to the time the magazine was at the printer. In today's digital world, the speed at which this layout was produced is less awe-inspiring, but for the time it was incredible. The film was transported to New York, where it was chemically developed, then checked to insure the quality of the shoot. The magazine layout was produced by hand for the printer, print proofs were collected and approved, then the photo essay was inserted into the magazine package and printed. Kennedy was sworn in only days before the issue hit the newsstands in the last week of January.

The first family's photographs are strikingly different from the other photographs in the magazine, including Avedon's images of Russian pianist Sviatoslav Richter. The Richter portraits reflect Avedon's noncommercial style. They use a stark white background; they offer a sense of the gentle pianist's inner life. They are unheroic images that expose his humanity. The Kennedy images, though, cannot be clearly defined as editorial photographs. They were noncommercial, but not purely personal, as they were assigned by a magazine.

Avedon's commercial work was driven by a client's needs and desires. The noncommercial work—predominately portraiture, but sometimes documentary—was guided by his quest to find the emotions and intellect that lay beneath his subject's surface. Sometimes the revelation was reflective of the sitter's inner world; sometimes it was reflective of Avedon's view of the larger human condition.

In a 1975 interview with Sally Quinn for the *Washington Post*, Avedon complained about his struggle to make the "crossover"—that photograph where he could "photograph a model as a human." The Kennedy photographs are the rare images where Avedon does produce a "crossover" success. For those photos, he drew on the flattering lighting and styling of a fashion spread that would be consistent within *Harper's Bazaar*'s pages. From his personal ideas about portraiture, he watched for and captured the moments that revealed something deeper about the Kennedys. He further shaped his ideas about the incoming president and his family through the arrangement of the photographs in the layout. This highly honed skill is illustrated over and over again as one evaluates Avedon's contact sheets, makes a personal selection, then compares it to Avedon's choice.

The six images that were published in *Harper's Bazaar* present the Kennedys as both idealized and vulnerable. Like the grand academic paintings by beaux arts painters such as Jacques-Louis David and Jean-Auguste-Dominique Ingres, these photographs are able to portray the individual on a personal level while representing larger themes

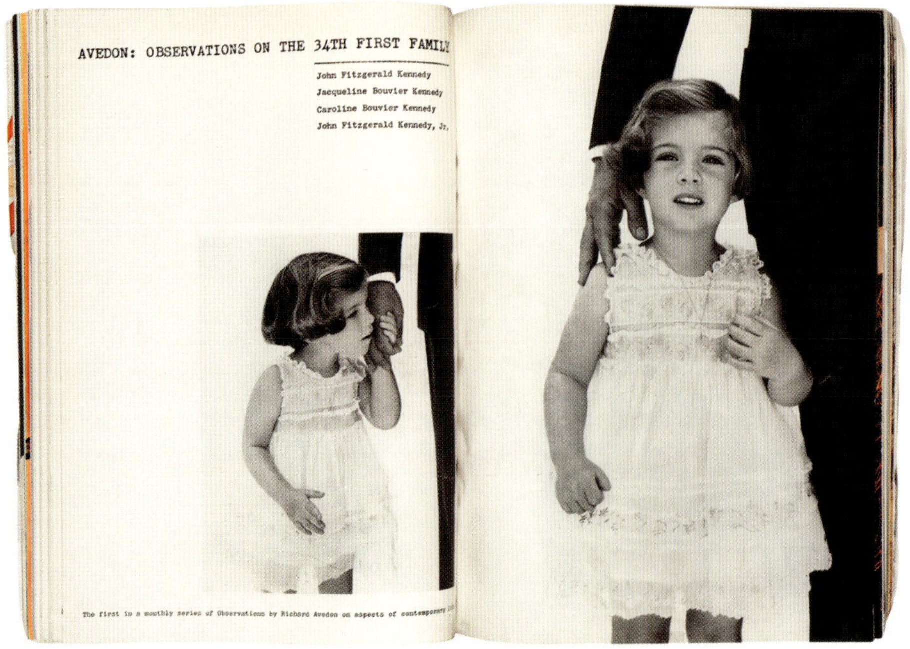

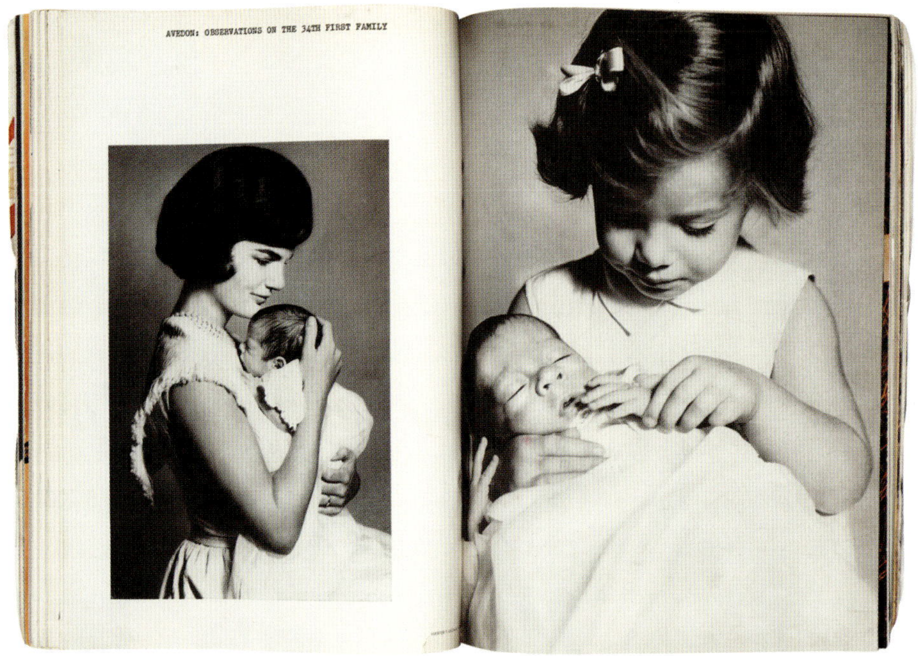

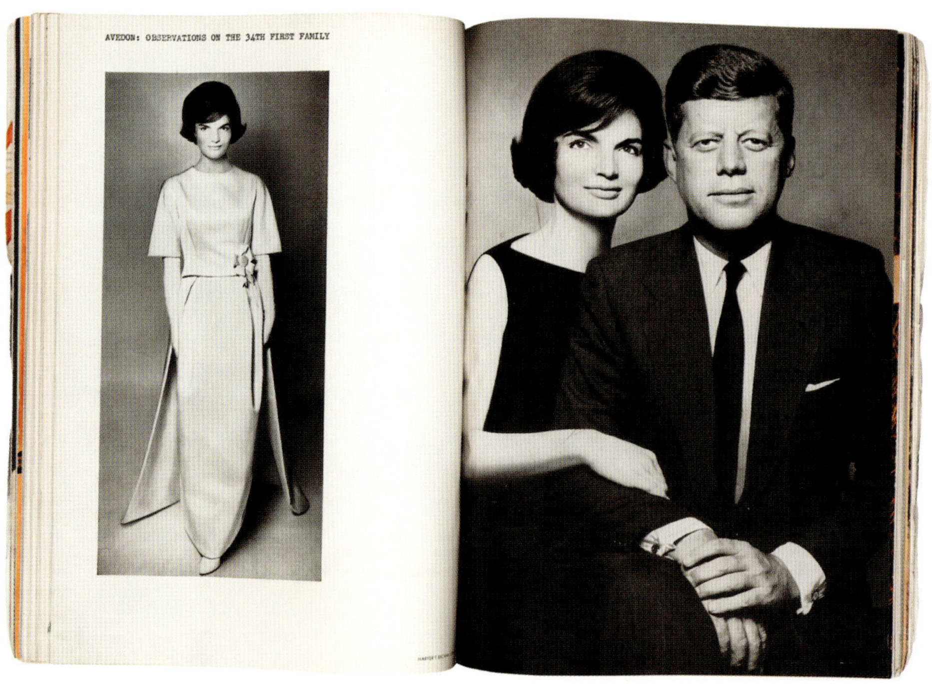

The final spreads of the Kennedys as they were published in Richard Avedon's *Observations* series in *Harper's Bazaar*, February 1961.

such as love, hope, security, and confidence. Ordered as they are, the photographs might be interpreted as images that are trying to instill a sense of confidence in the reader towards the Kennedy presidency, particularly as they were made during an era in which people still believed authority figures had the power to make individual lives better, having yet to experience the turmoil of the 1960s that would turn this sentiment on its head. Prefacing his forty-page portfolio "Exiles: The Kennedy Court at the End of the American Century" in *The New Yorker*, Avedon wrote, "In January of 1961, just before John Kennedy's Inauguration, I did a series of portraits of him and his family at their house in Palm Beach. The Kennedys and many of the people they attracted were full of promise and pride, and they had a respect for intellect that I haven't seen again in American politics. From July 8th to September 4th of this year [1993], I traveled across the country to photograph surviving men and women of that period—people mostly of my generation, who for a while had faith in power."

Through the first pair of photographs, the reader establishes an emotional connection to Kennedy; through the second pair, a sense of nurturing and comfort; through the third, confidence that Kennedy will be a good president.

The first photographs of Caroline and Kennedy are endearing without being overly sentimental. Caroline's sweet gesture of holding her father's hand to her face captures the essence of a child's unconditional love and the intense desire to have that love returned. Many readers, taken by Caroline's heartfelt gesture, would have felt a connection to the photograph from that perspective as well as transferred their own feelings of adoration toward Kennedy. Represented by his hand and his leg only, Kennedy is in a sense abstracted here—a symbol of paternal nationalism. In the paired photograph, Caroline stands within the compositional triangle of her father's leg and arm. His fingers hold her shoulder at the triangle's apex, enfolding her, protecting her from the stranger taking her picture. Similarly, the viewer can imagine Kennedy protecting America from danger.

The second pair of images, featuring Jackie and the children, reinforces these feelings of comfort. Beautiful and maternal, graceful and nurturing, the photo of Jackie portrays her as a devoted, loving mother—values she would hopefully apply as first lady. In art history, a baby symbolically represents hope for the future. Here, six-week-old John Jr. fulfills that role, his tiny, pale hand reaching toward Caroline's arm for security. The photographs of John and Caroline ask the viewer to embrace the new years of leadership.

The final pair of photographs presents the public face of Jackie and Kennedy. In her pre-inaugural gown, Jackie engages the viewer with a mix of restraint and challenge. In this regal portrait, she projects her ability to hold court. In the final photograph, Jackie sits comfortably, but resolutely, behind the solid, confident president-elect. The same woman who can command authority also knows her place as a wife, the role of many of *Harper's Bazaar*'s readers at the time. In these images, she sits behind Kennedy. With her arm over his, she is physically linked to him, signaling his leadership status and her inseparable support as his wife. In that final photograph, Kennedy appears as a full human figure, not as a fractured representation of himself. He seems calm, comfortable, and self-assured. The Kennedys' directness and sincerity enlist the reader's support and confidence.

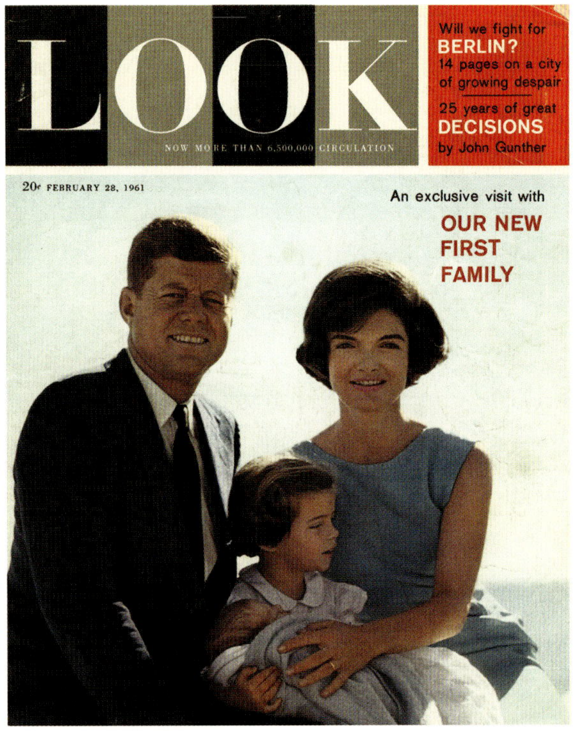

The final spreads of the Kennedys as they were published in *LOOK*, February 28, 1961.

LOOK and the Associated Press

Avedon's photographs for the *LOOK* article, "An Informal Visit with Our New First Family," are stylistically and functionally different from the ones for *Harper's Bazaar*. First and most obviously, they are outdoor action photographs using natural light, and a number of them are in color. The *Harper's Bazaar* images had neither a group portrait of the four family members nor, with the exception of three frames, a series of photographs with Jackie and Caroline together. The *LOOK* images were part of the magazine's cover story. The color image of the first family on the cover is informal, and the interiors are meant to capture the family at play, giving us an inside look at them at home. But the photos do not idealize them in the same way that the *Harper's Bazaar* images do. While the *Harper's Bazaar* images were manipulated to create an eloquent graphic effect emphasizing the photographer's vision, the *LOOK* pictures were presented more casually—they were snapshotlike. With eleven black-and-white and color photographs, the *LOOK* layout is much looser, longer, and more varied.

The text for the article was written by *LOOK* editor and noted journalist Laura Bergquist. In November 1960, she published interviews with both Fidel Castro and Che Guevara, so it's somewhat surprising that she would then pen a flowery text to accompany Avedon's photographs. However, having published many Kennedy images and worked extensively with *LOOK* photographer Stanley Tretick, she was aware of the Kennedys' desire to be seen as a perfect family. She also recognized the need to maintain a working relationship with the president and his press managers for future access. Although the photographic essay was not a political exposé, but a fun, lively view of the new president and his family, she understood the value of the article to *LOOK*'s readership.

Perhaps the most informative photograph published in the *LOOK* article is of Jackie and Caroline sitting on the window seat playing with dolls. In the background, one can see Kennedy walking towards the house after a swim in the ocean. Considered from the broad perspective of the era, the image would have appealed to many of the magazine's readers. Jackie and Caroline, framed by the vertical lines of the curtain and the horizontal lines of the window seat and cushion, are part of the domestic sphere of child rearing, even seeming to coach the next generation of females on child care through play. The president-elect, seen through the window and framed by two palm trees, exemplifies outdoor ruggedness and good health. Readers knew that the Kennedys' luxuries exceeded their own, yet Avedon's images make it seem as if they held the same family standards as the rest of the country.

This photograph echoes Jackie's self-positioning as a supportive wife and doting mother, rather than as politician. "I'll do everything I can and should do in an official way. But I don't want my young children brought up by nurses and Secret Service men," she said in a post-election press conference. On December 11, 1960, just weeks after John Jr.'s birth, she wrote in an article for the *Times-Herald*: "Maybe if you start with love, security and discipline and just work from there, being sensitive to your child's developing interests, the 'raising' would be more rewarding all around—and infinitely more fun. Children have imagination, a quality that seems to flicker out in so many adults. That is why it is such a joy to be with children."

Other "typical family" and joy-filled photographs in the article include mother and daughter outside on the lawn, Caroline running, and another casual portrait of the family. The article informs the reader that Caroline

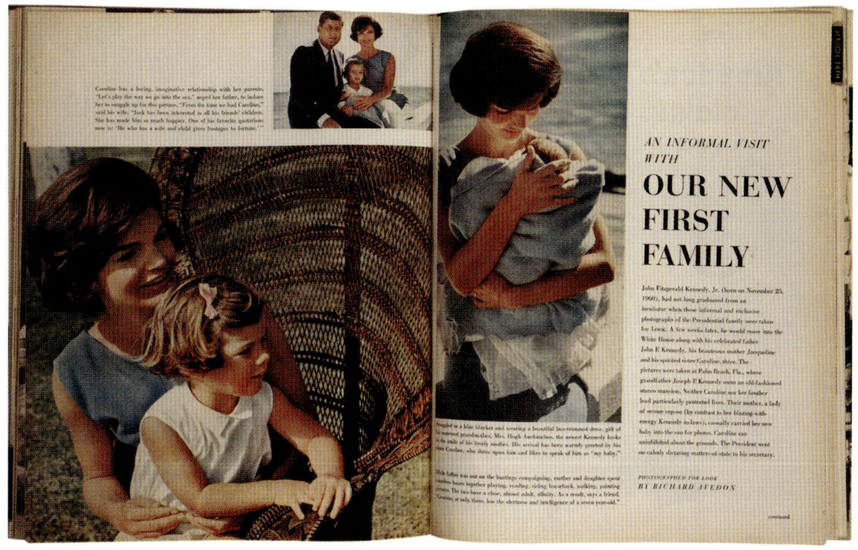

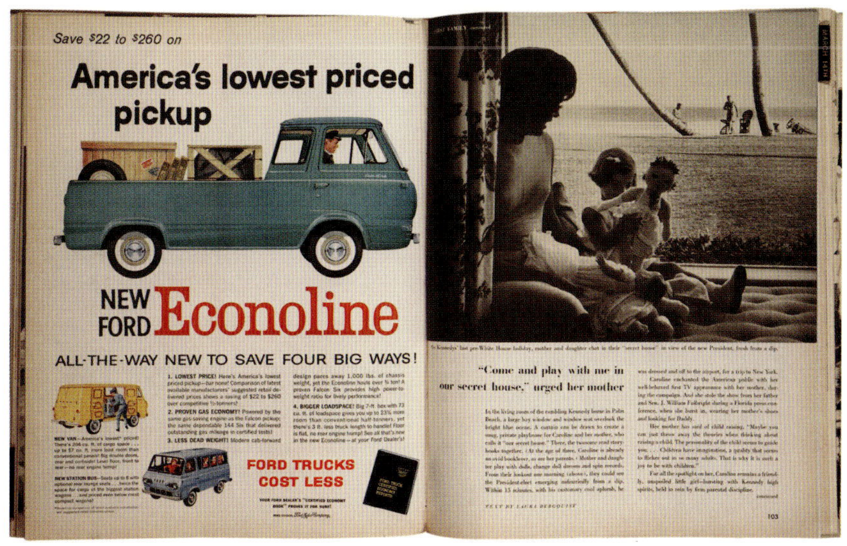

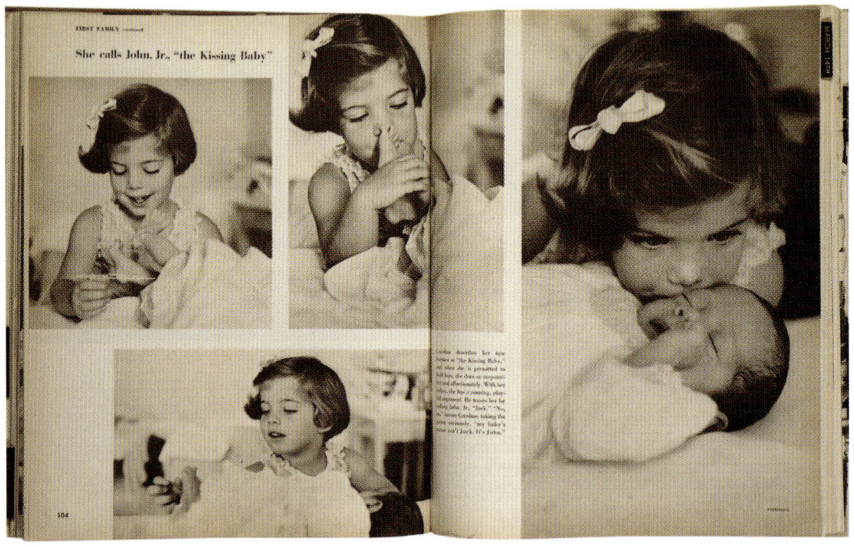

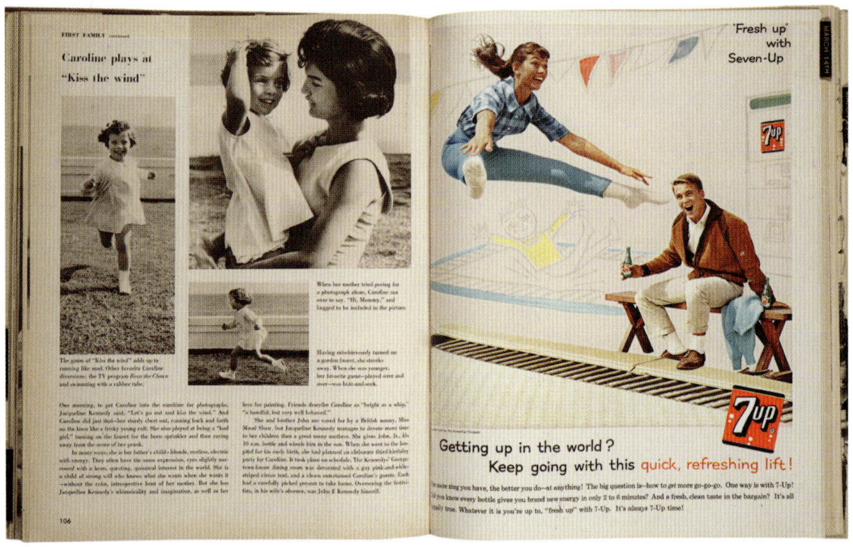

calls her little brother "the Kissing Baby." The photos show her playing with and kissing his feet and face. These photographs ran in the *Washington Post* on February 14, 1961. Smaller selections of photographs appeared in newspapers in Los Angeles, Chicago, and New Orleans.

Unlike the enlarged *Harper's Bazaar* contact sheets in the Smithsonian's collection, the *LOOK* contact sheets are marked up. With these contact sheets, one can peek into John Jr.'s room and see the baby scale and the ornate lamp on the night stand in addition to viewing alternative shots and the cropping selections. Because these are among her private papers, Jackie probably had a hand in selecting which images appeared in *LOOK* or were released to the Associated Press and other news agencies.

The release of the *LOOK* photographs to the public may have been prompted by a noisy United Press International editor. On February 1, 1961, Frank Tremaine complained in a letter to Kennedy's press secretary, Pierre Salinger, about a lack of access to Avedon's photographs of the president and his family for use by news organizations. He wrote that he believed it was inappropriate for a commercial photographer to profit financially or gain personal publicity from the photographs of the president and his family. Several news reporters followed up on Tremaine's complaints during press conferences, with Salinger more or less dismissing the questions. Ultimately, though, the White House did release twenty-one of the Avedon photos to the Associated Press. The images appeared in newspapers across the country. Some of the photographs were retained for use as White House hand-outs—pictures that could be sent to citizens requesting a photo of

Caroline or John Jr. It's very likely that some of these photographs are still preserved in private scrapbooks and photo albums.

By the end of February 1961, the Kennedy administration was settling into place and Americans were responding to the new president's actions rather than responding to pre-inaugural media. Other photographers began to satisfy the demand for new pictures of John Jr. and Caroline, and the distribution of Avedon's portraits of the children came to an end. Once *LOOK* was off the newsstands, the photographs, contact sheets, and engraver's proofs were put away until Avedon donated the *Harper's Bazaar* materials to the Smithsonian in 1966. The *LOOK* materials were rediscovered in Jackie's papers while doing research for this book in 2006.

At the time of John F. Kennedy's assassination and for several years after, hundreds of magazine articles and books were published about the event and the family. Certainly, Avedon could have allowed his images to be used in any number of memorial photography books, especially because his were the only formal pre-inaugural pictures. But he chose not to rerelease his photographs. In fact, the day after the assassination, Avedon walked around New York City photographing people carrying a newspaper with the headline "Kennedy Is Dead." For Avedon, Kennedy's death was not an opportunity to profit, but a time of reflection and concern for the nation. Throughout the 1960s and into the 1970s, Avedon participated in a number of civil rights marches, signed petitions, donated photographs for fund raisers for veterans of the Vietnam War, and even got arrested while continuing to carry out this concern for the issues affecting the country.

When Avedon donated his pre-inaugural photographs of the Kennedys to the Smithsonian, his work joined other collections of American political, fashion, and photographic history as well as donations from the Kennedy family. These important artifacts have additional resonance because their iconic creators and users chose to leave them for future historians to evaluate. Exploring the background and meaning of Richard Avedon's photographs of the Kennedys allows for a better understanding of the photographer and his work as well as that small window of history between Kennedy's election and the start of his administration.

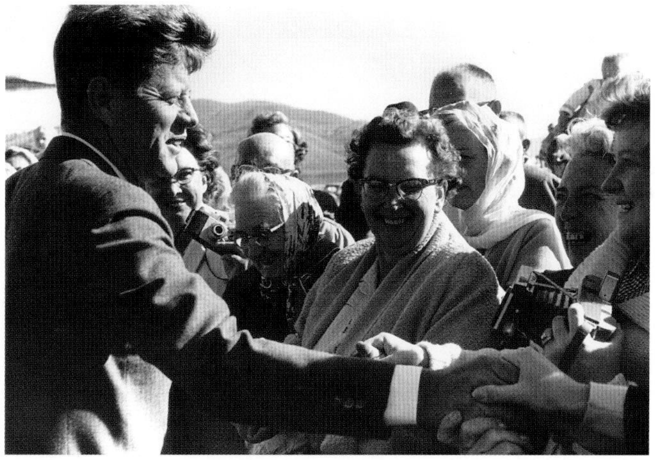

President Kennedy shakes hands with members of the public, 1963.

THE ART OF AVEDON'S PHOTOGRAPHY

To get a satisfactory print, one that contains all you intended, is very often more difficult and dangerous than the sitting itself.
—Richard Avedon, *Observations*, 1959

In the mid-twentieth century, a "good" photographic print was often defined by photographers, photography editors, curators, collectors, and dealers by comparing it to the work of Ansel Adams, Minor White, and Edward Weston. Adams' style of photography, often known as "straight photography," has inspired untold numbers of photographers. This style intends to maximize the technical possibilities of photographic materials, so that the blacks are true blacks, the whites are true whites, and there is a great range of gray tones in between. This approach to photography lends itself well to landscapes and other images in which there's a sense of capturing "reality."

Avedon's photographs indicate that he has no need of or desire for straight photography's heightened reference to real-world actualities. In 1997, he told a *New York Times* reporter, "There is no such thing as photographic reality." He was interested in making photographs that were psychologically stirring. To do that, he manipulated his negatives and prints. Adams once described negatives as scores of music that could be interpreted and reinterpreted. Avedon's negatives, however, become the basis for photographs that were treated more like canvases wet with oil paint.

Richard Avedon's *Observations*, published in 1959 with text by Truman Capote, provides insight to his working methods. That book shares more than a title with the series of photographic essays in *Harper's Bazaar*. Stylistically similar, the full-bleed photographs are accompanied by minimal text and significant white space. In the book, Capote quotes Avedon: "When I'm photographing, I immediately know when I've got the image I really want. But to get the image out of the camera and into the open is another matter. I make as many as sixty prints of a picture, would make a hundred if it would mean a fraction's improvement, help show the invisible, the inside out." The negatives and prints on these pages are an opportunity to explore what Avedon meant.

Getting the Image Out of the Camera

Examining Avedon's contact sheets and comparing the many images there to the ultimate image Avedon selects offers some insight to his intentions. This contact sheet in which Jackie is holding John Jr. is a good example. Following conventional rules about portraiture, the center photograph in the bottom row showing Jackie slightly smiling and looking at the camera would be a natural choice because she appears happy and is directly engaging the viewer.

The image at left in the bottom row shows Jackie holding John Jr. about as tightly as a mother can; his nose is even a little smashed to her chest. She's cradling him in a way to protect him and to hold him close. Although Avedon is looking to "show the invisible," in this case a mother's love, the baby's head hides too much of Jackie's face. The emotions have gone too far, overwhelming the photograph and leaving no psychological or physical tension. Avedon takes a step back from this intimate moment and avoids sentimentality by selecting the second image in the first column for the *Harper's Bazaar* spread.

The chosen photograph shows Jackie looking slightly beyond John Jr. while still holding him close. Her chin and his head are just touching. His face is barely above the surface of her dress. She cradles his head, but grips his body. The result is a more complex portrait of Jackie: a beautiful, intelligent woman and a loving, protective mother. This image was the third picture in the series of photographs selected for *Harper's Bazaar*.

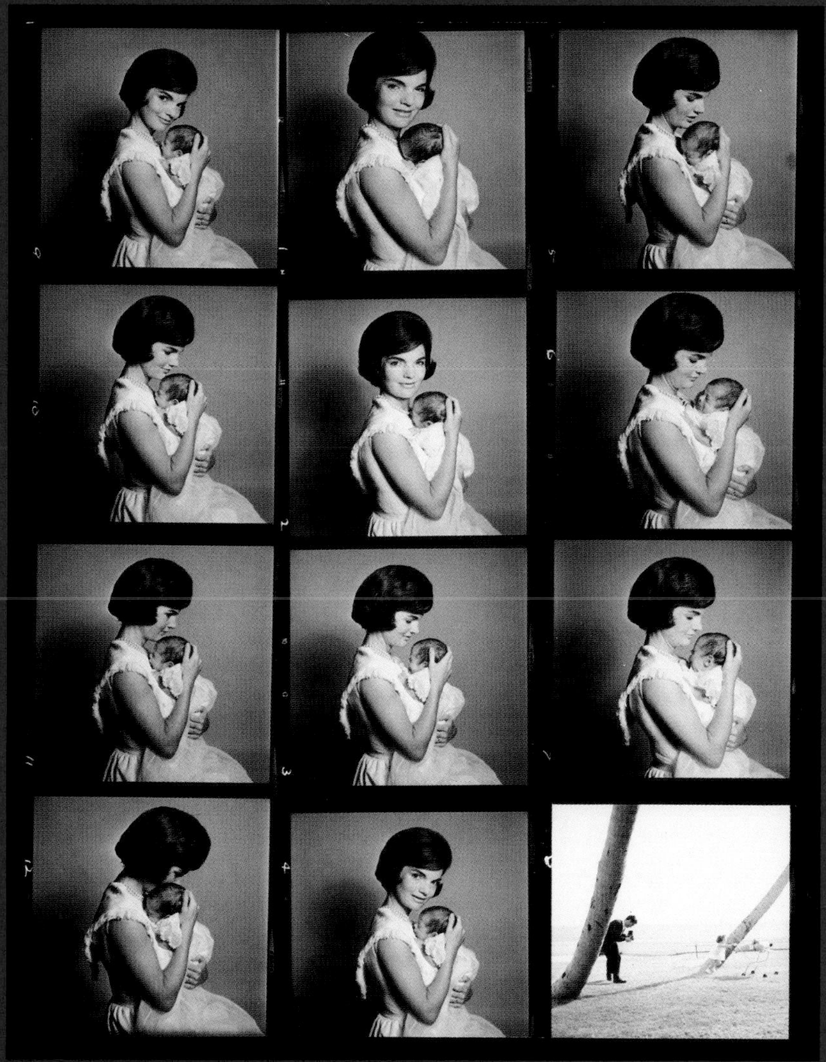

Show the Invisible, the Inside Out

Avedon's ability to move a portrait beyond a mere physical resemblance of the sitter has as much to do with the original exposure of the negative and image selection as it does with his printing choices. Not only does he capture the moment and select his image, but he also prints the photograph in a way that emphasizes or underscores his intent. On page 36, the photograph of Jackie and John F. Kennedy seated on a bench where Jackie's ring finger is bent illustrates this point.

Compare the digital scan from the original 2¼-inch negative to the final print. Looking at the scan, it is easy to see that the negative started out evenly exposed. To achieve a gray background with the existing white paper background in this photograph, Avedon turns down his lights while taking the picture. The result creates a more sculptural image of the sitters.

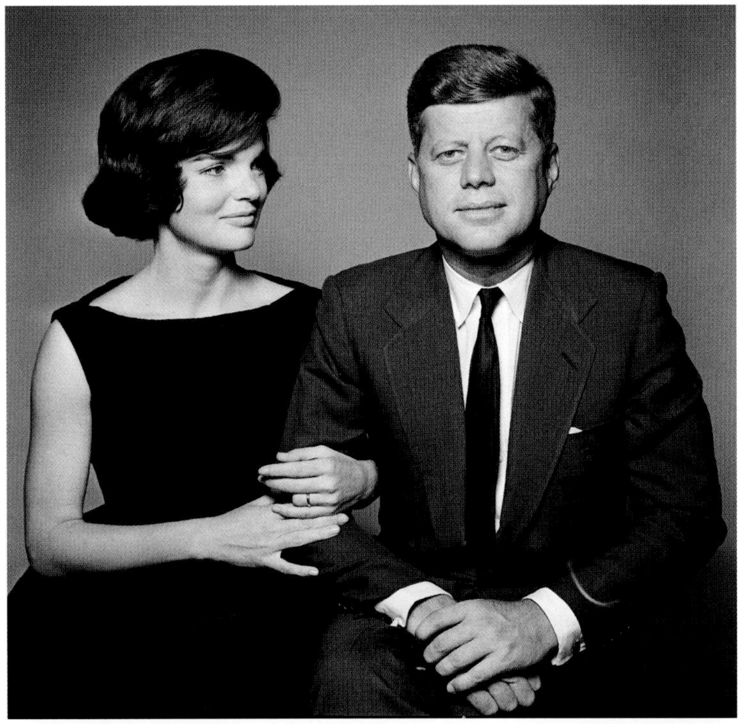

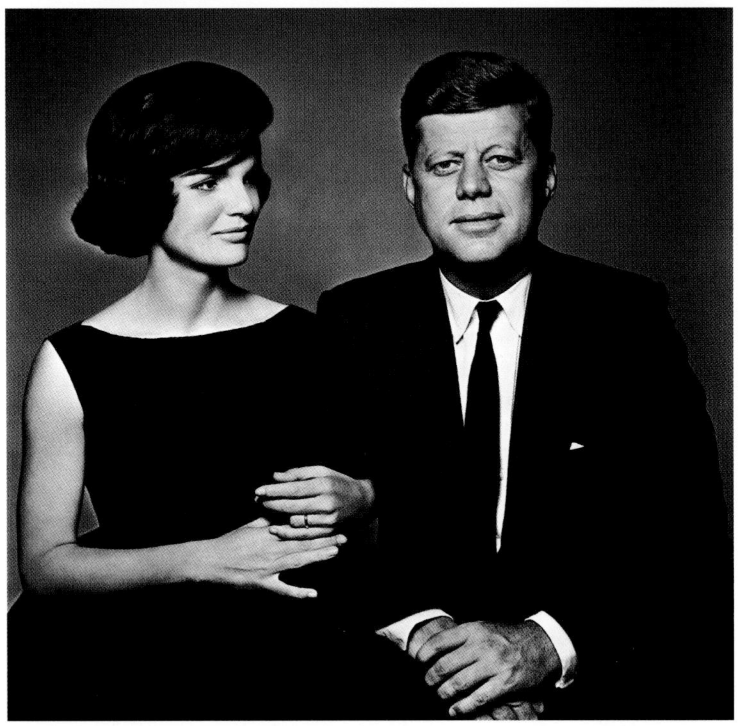

The top image is a digital scan from Avedon's original 2¼-inch negative. Below it is Avedon's final version of the photograph.

When the film was processed, it was rolled onto a metal reel. A darkroom assistant accidentally bent the film, which caused the half-moon on John F. Kennedy's sleeve. The halo around Jackie's hair is bromide drag, which occurs when the negative and the developing chemicals are not kept in enough motion. If this happens, there is an excess of bromide created along an edge where darks and lights meet and overexposes the light side. These are both fairly common darkroom mishaps.

Most photographers utilize dodging and burning techniques to modifying the negative's exposure to the photographic paper. Generally, this is done to even out the tonal qualities or bring out details in a negative. Under the enlarger, Avedon's photographs experienced quite a bit of controlled dodging and burning to move the print towards his vision of the final image. Avedon guided the printing of his photographs by giving instructions to his printers to shape the specific details and nuances in his photographs.

In this photograph, he uses dodging and burning for two purposes—first for practical reasons, second for aesthetic ones. In the original negative, the light is cast evenly across the couple. By darkening the area on Kennedy's sleeve, the bright half-moon is dimmed. However, the print becomes so dark that the pattern in Kennedy's suit and the texture of Jackie's dress are obliterated. This darkening encourages the viewer to focus on something other than the superficial details of the fabric.

Through dodging and burning, Avedon lightens Jackie's skin so that she almost looks like a porcelain sculpture. The overall lighting in the photograph is also redirected so that it highlights Jackie's neck and both of the couple's hands.

Retouching is another technique that shapes the photograph for practical and aesthetic purposes. Here, Kennedy's wrinkles are softened. Jackie's neckline is sculpted by removing the dress along her back towards her shoulders. The left side of her face and hairline are softened. The overall effect of dodging, burning, and retouching removes details to focus on the sitters themselves, emphasizing Jackie's fragility and Kennedy's sturdiness. Although this image was considered for the *Harper's Bazaar* photography essay, it was ultimately omitted.

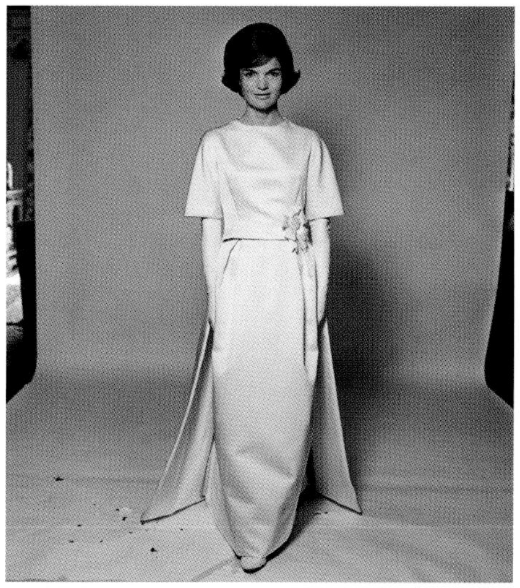

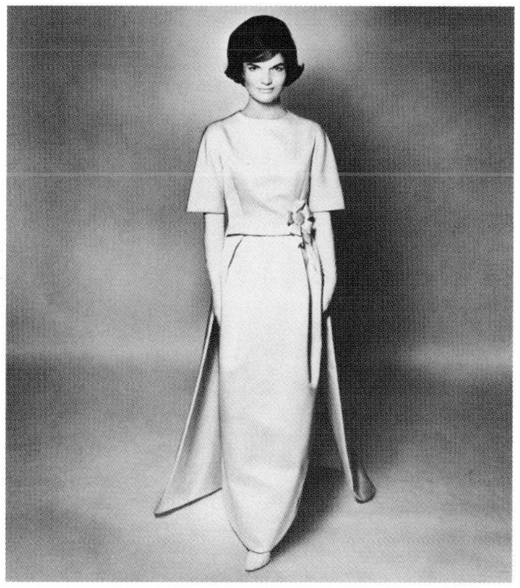

The third set of images (at right) demonstrates the more practical aspect of retouching. The final image appeared in *Harper's Bazaar* as the fifth photograph in the series. During the sitting of Jackie in her pre-inaugural gown, the heels of her shoes punctured the backdrop paper. Simply applying a matching gray tone to the negative removed the holes. In this case, a photographic print was made in which the holes appeared. An 11 x 14-inch copy negative was made of that photograph, then retouched before being sent to the printer. As part of the process, the printer sent back proof prints to Avedon and *Harper's Bazaar* for approval, then went on press. Proof prints for the *Harper's Bazaar* spread are in the Richard Avedon Collection at the Center for Creative Photography in Tucson, Arizona.

The following pages provide an opportunity to examine a selection of the Smithsonian collection of Richard Avedon's Kennedy photographs. There are sometimes striking differences in the look of the photographs because Avedon made only nine final prints of the 219 photographs in the collection. The square images are digital scans from the negatives represented on the contact sheets. They were printed as conventional photographs because there was no reason to attempt to print them with Avedon's aesthetic. The contact sheets and the rectangular images are printed as closely as possible to Avedon's version of the photographs. Taken with the information provided here and the reader's own perspective, the Smithsonian collection can be experienced in a unique, contextualized way.

THE PHOTOGRAPHS

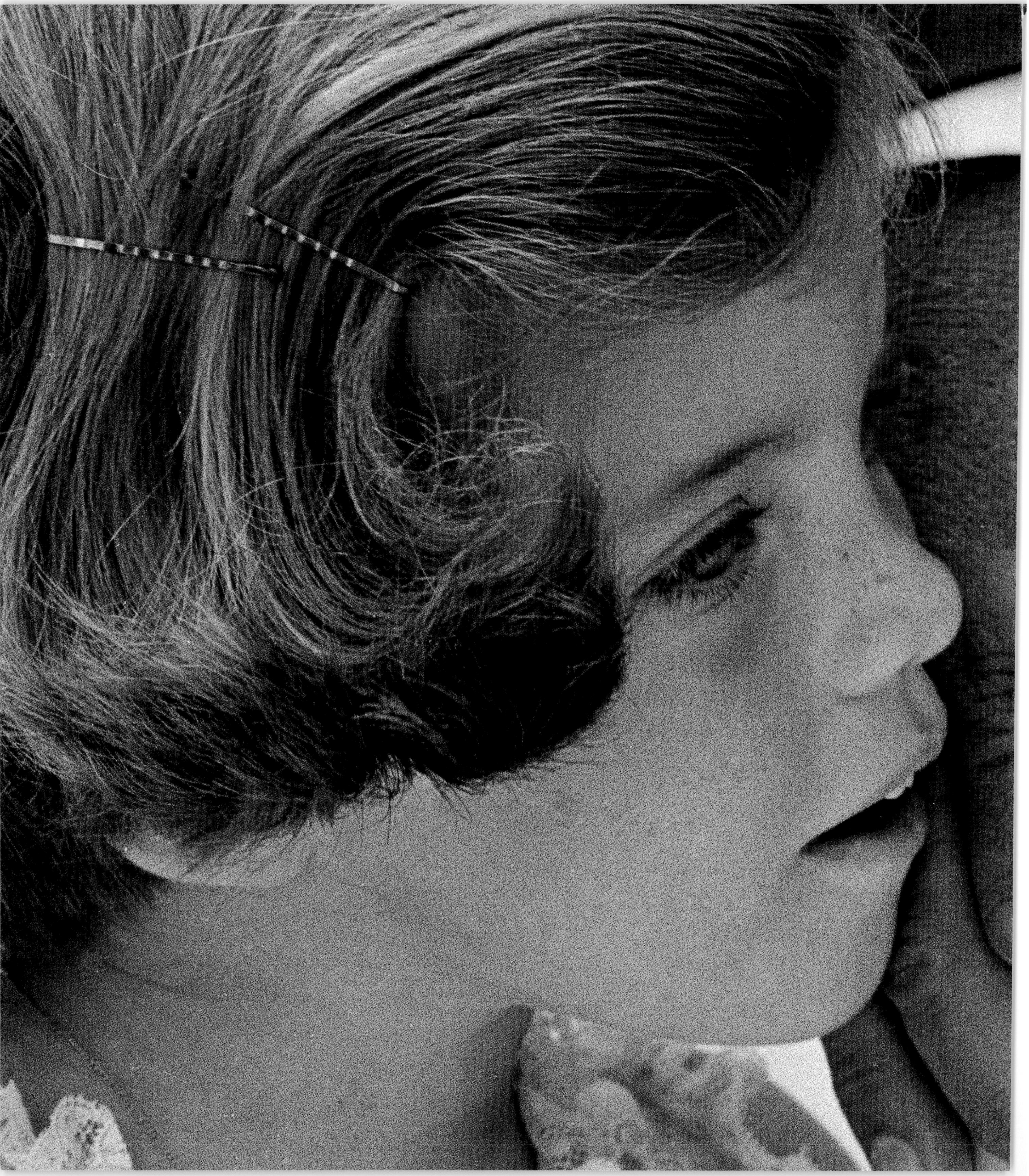

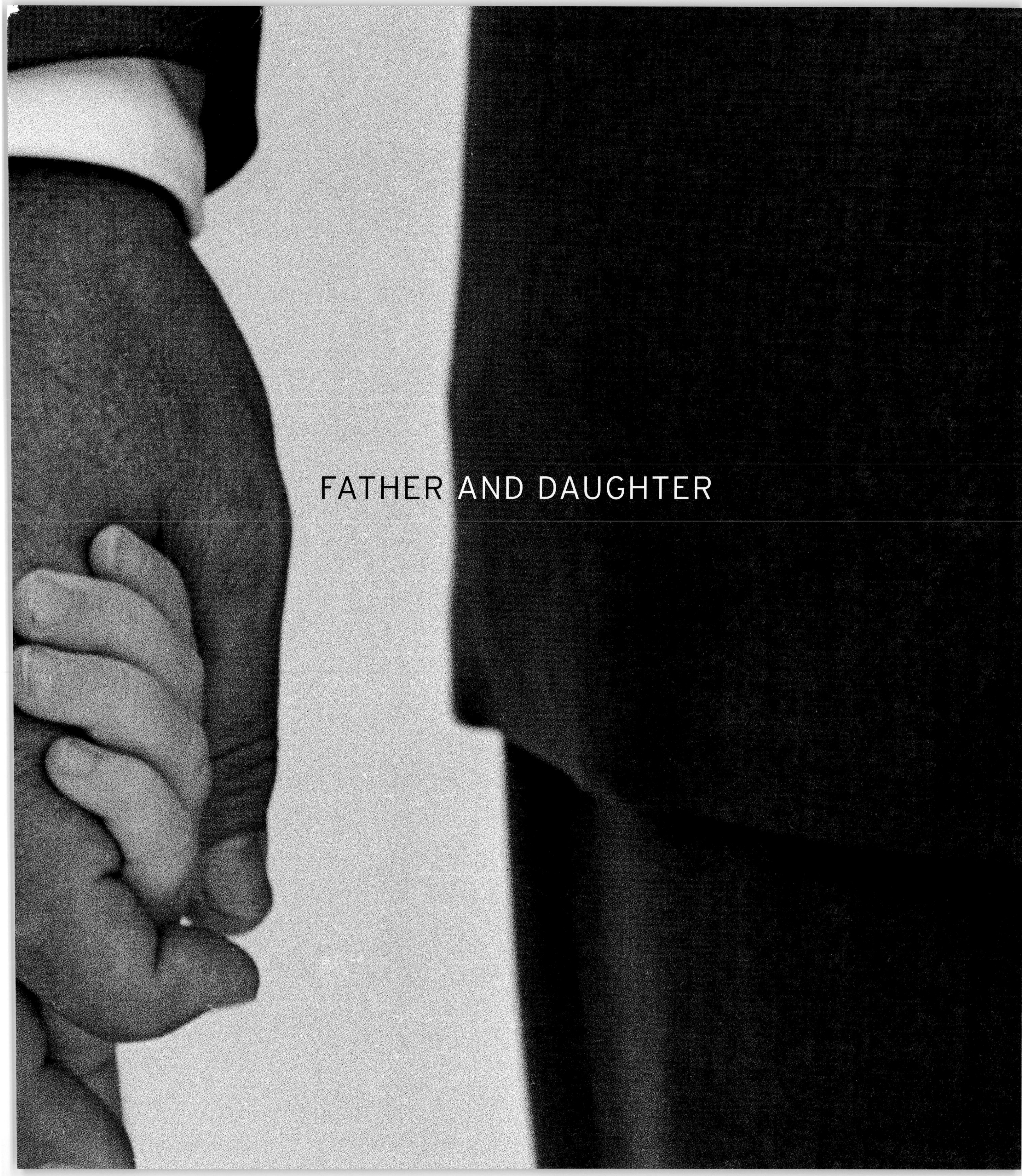
FATHER AND DAUGHTER

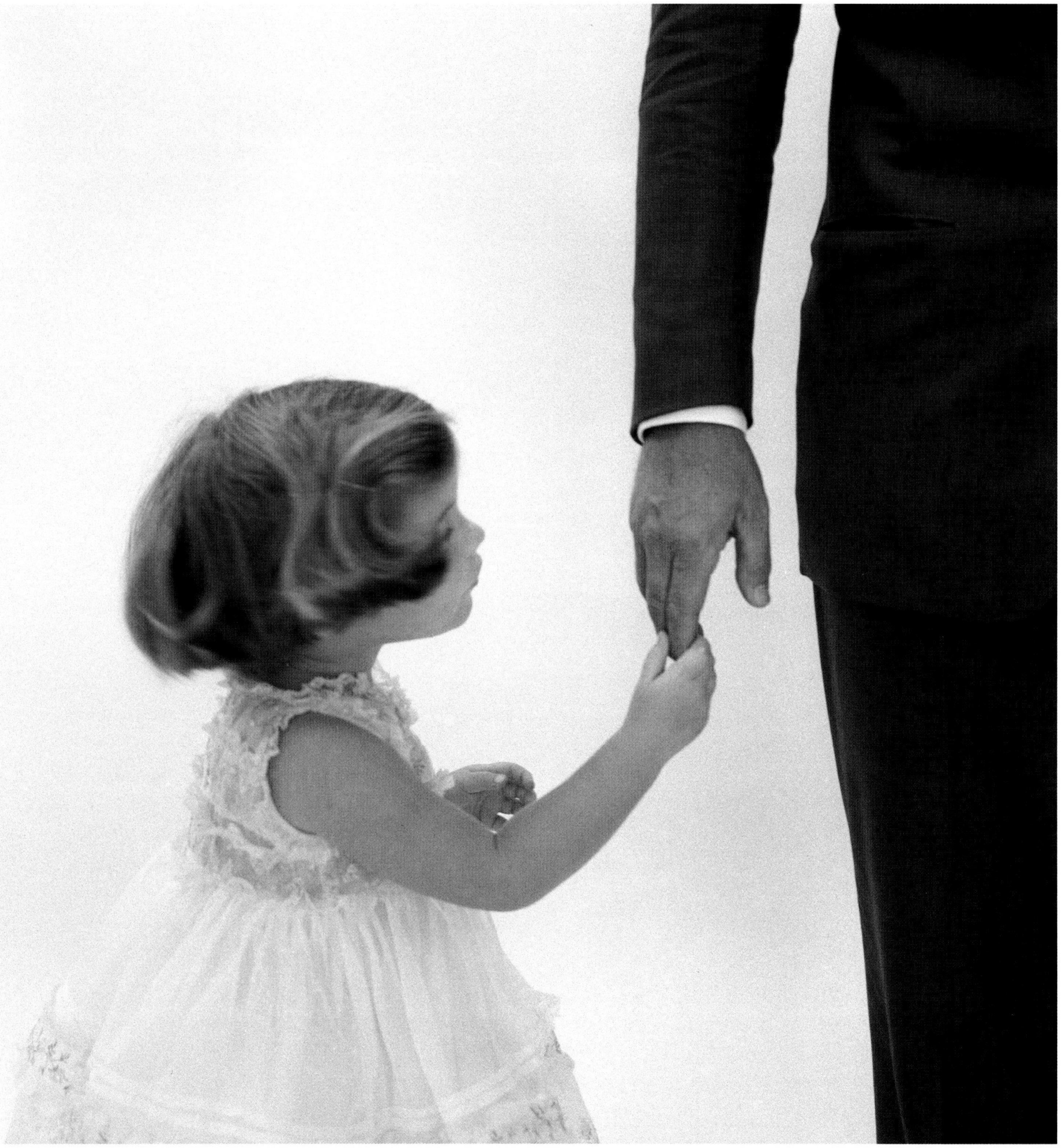

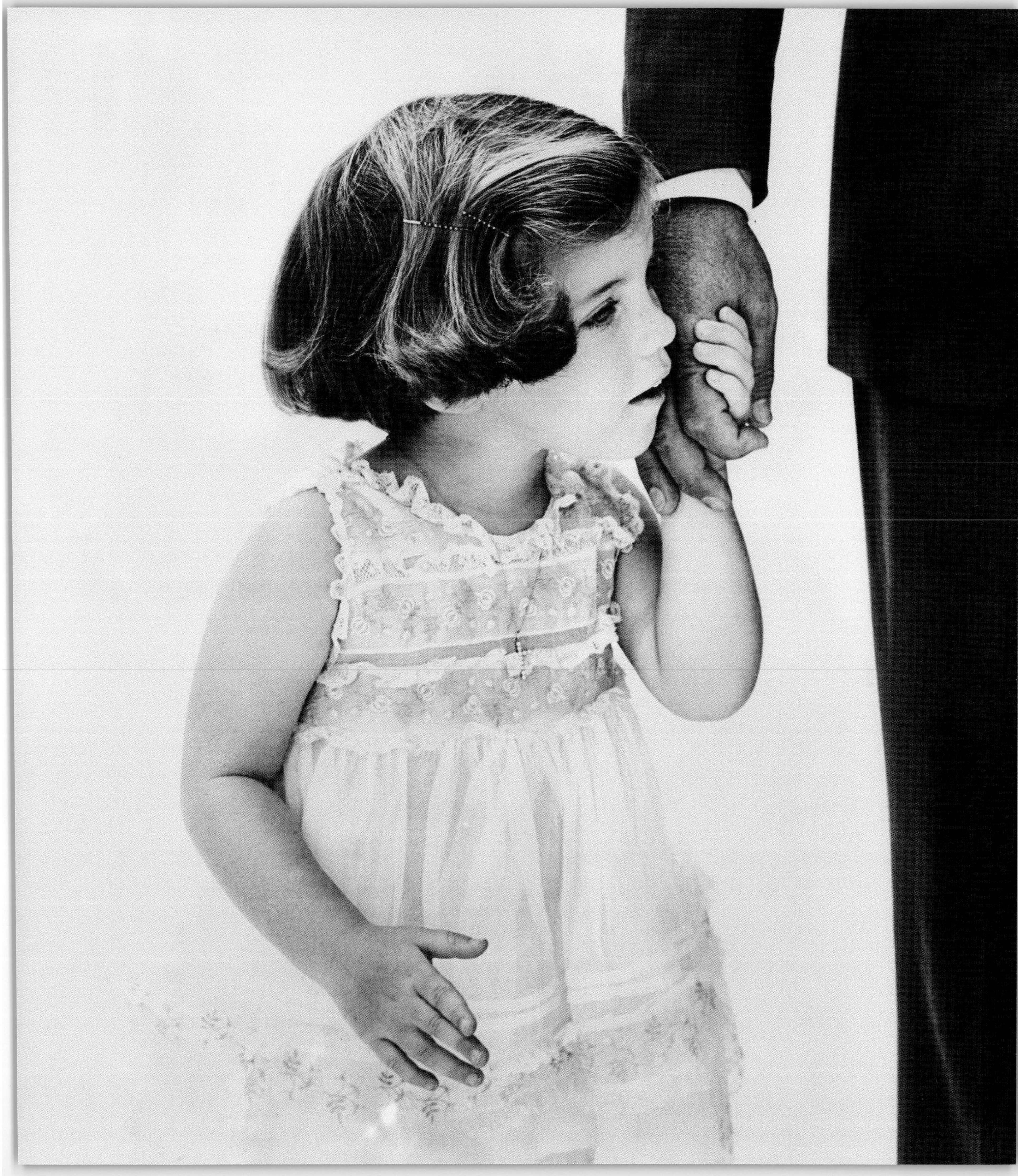

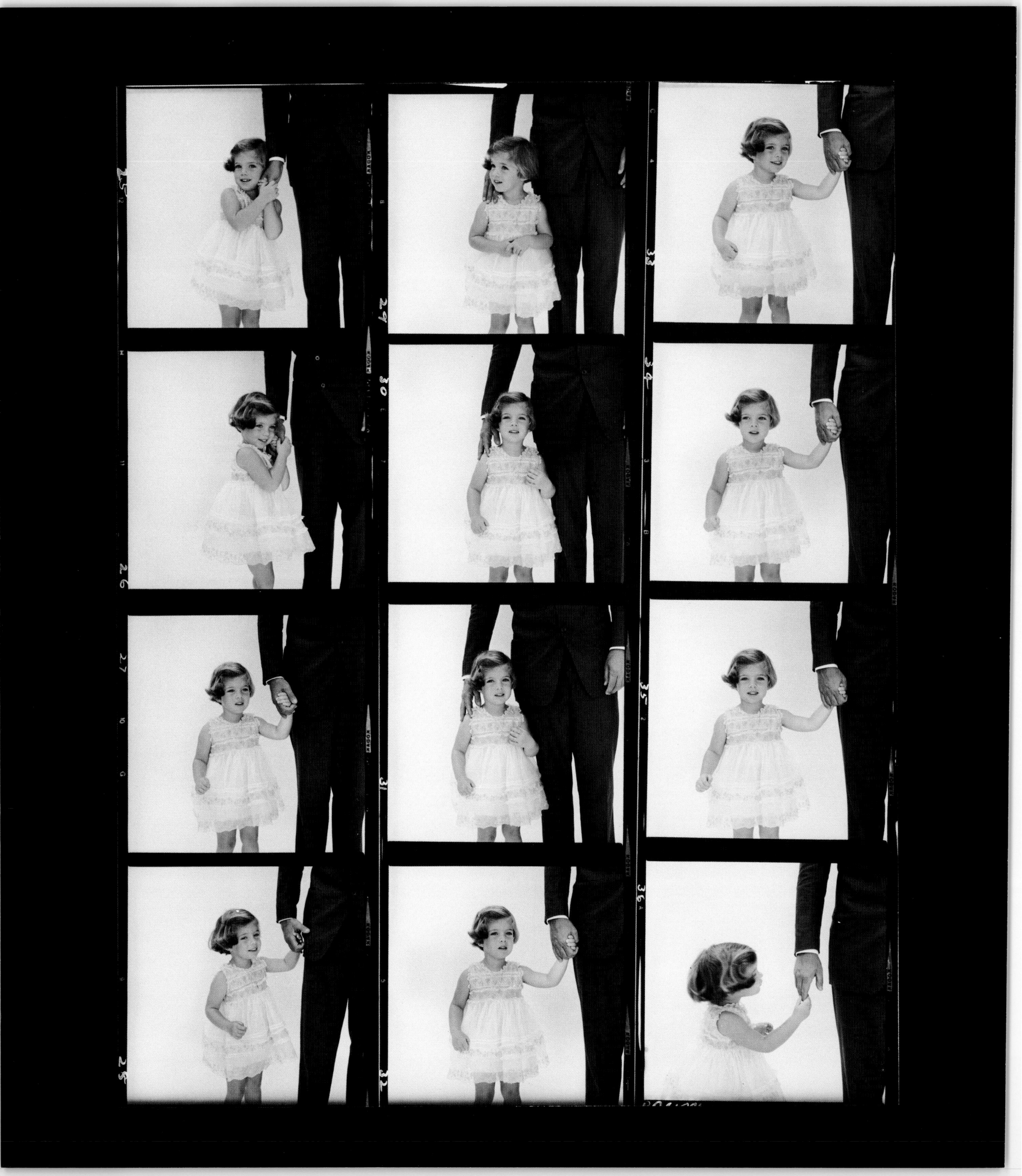

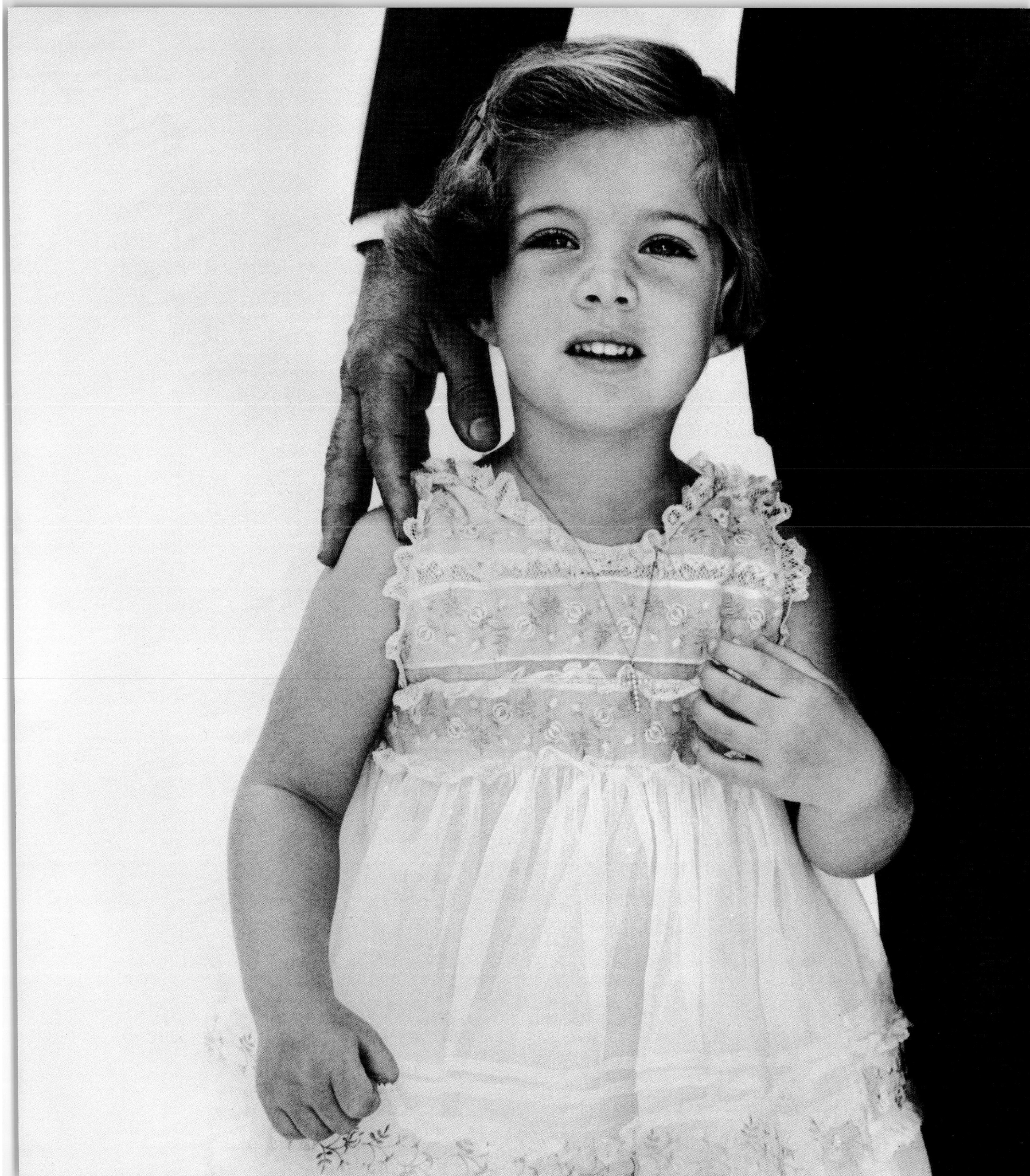

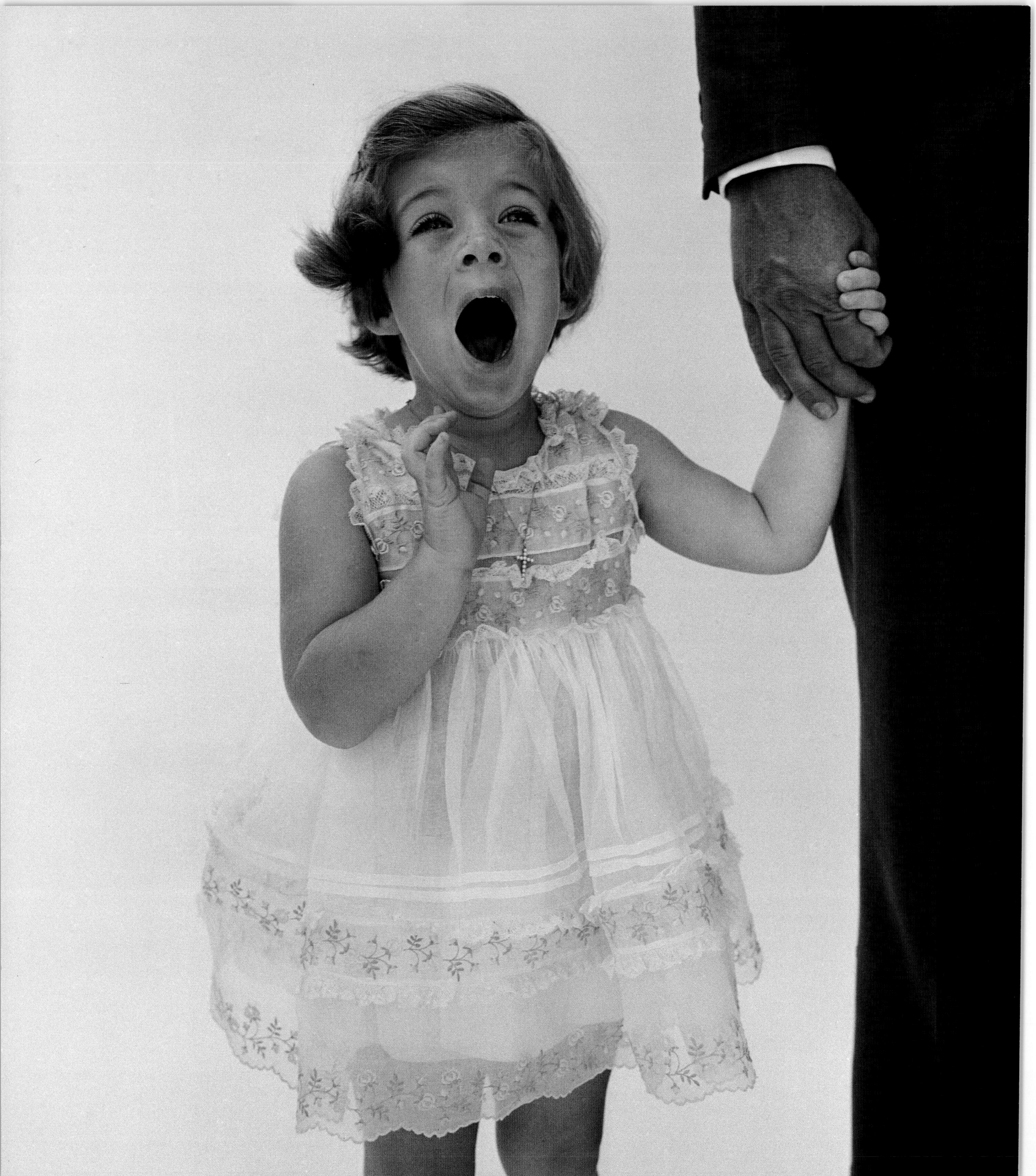

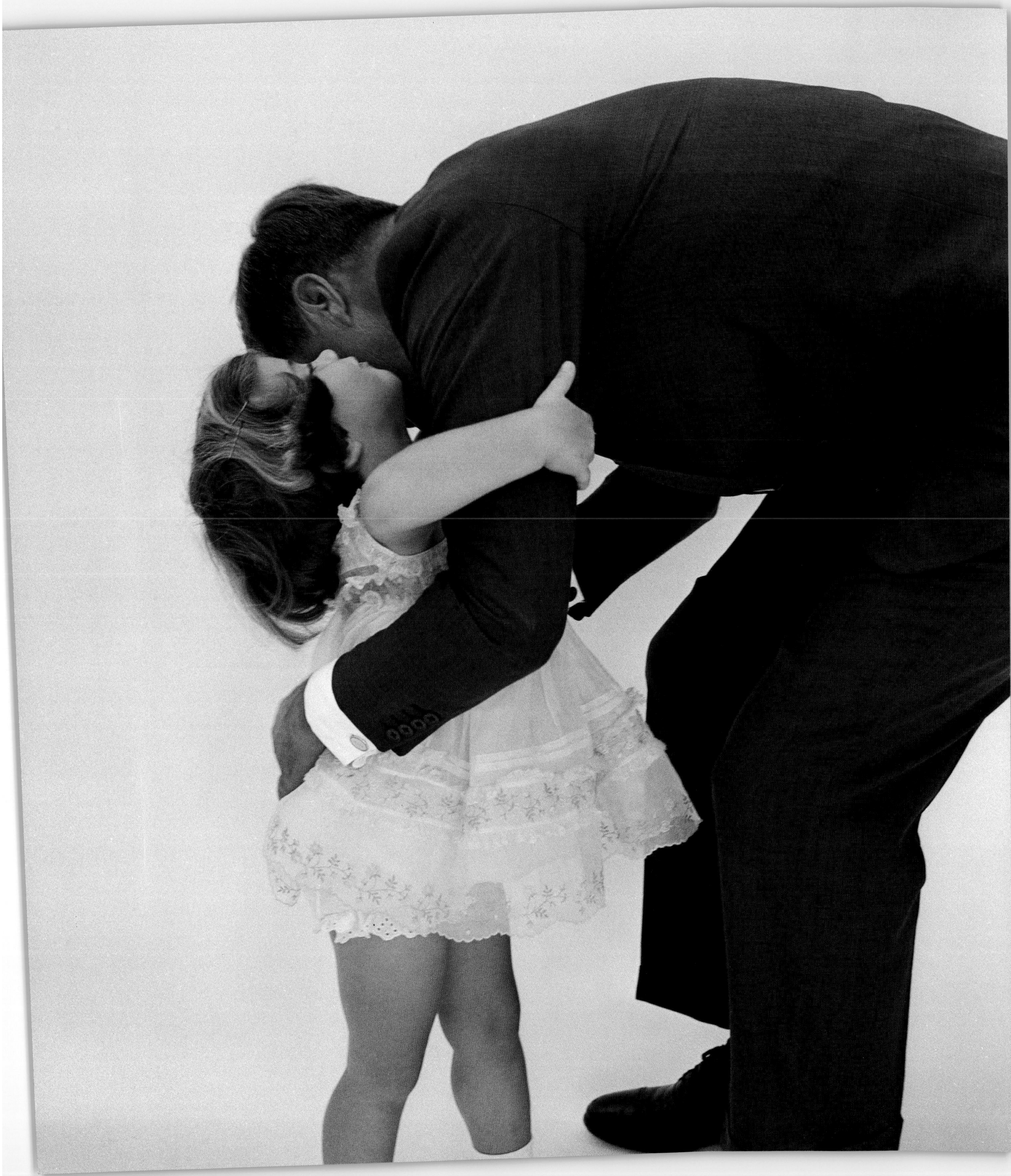

IN MANY WAYS, SHE IS HER FATHER'S CHILD—

blond, restless, electric with energy. They often have the same expression, eyes slightly narrowed with a keen, questing, quizzical interest in the world.

—*LOOK*, February 28, 1961

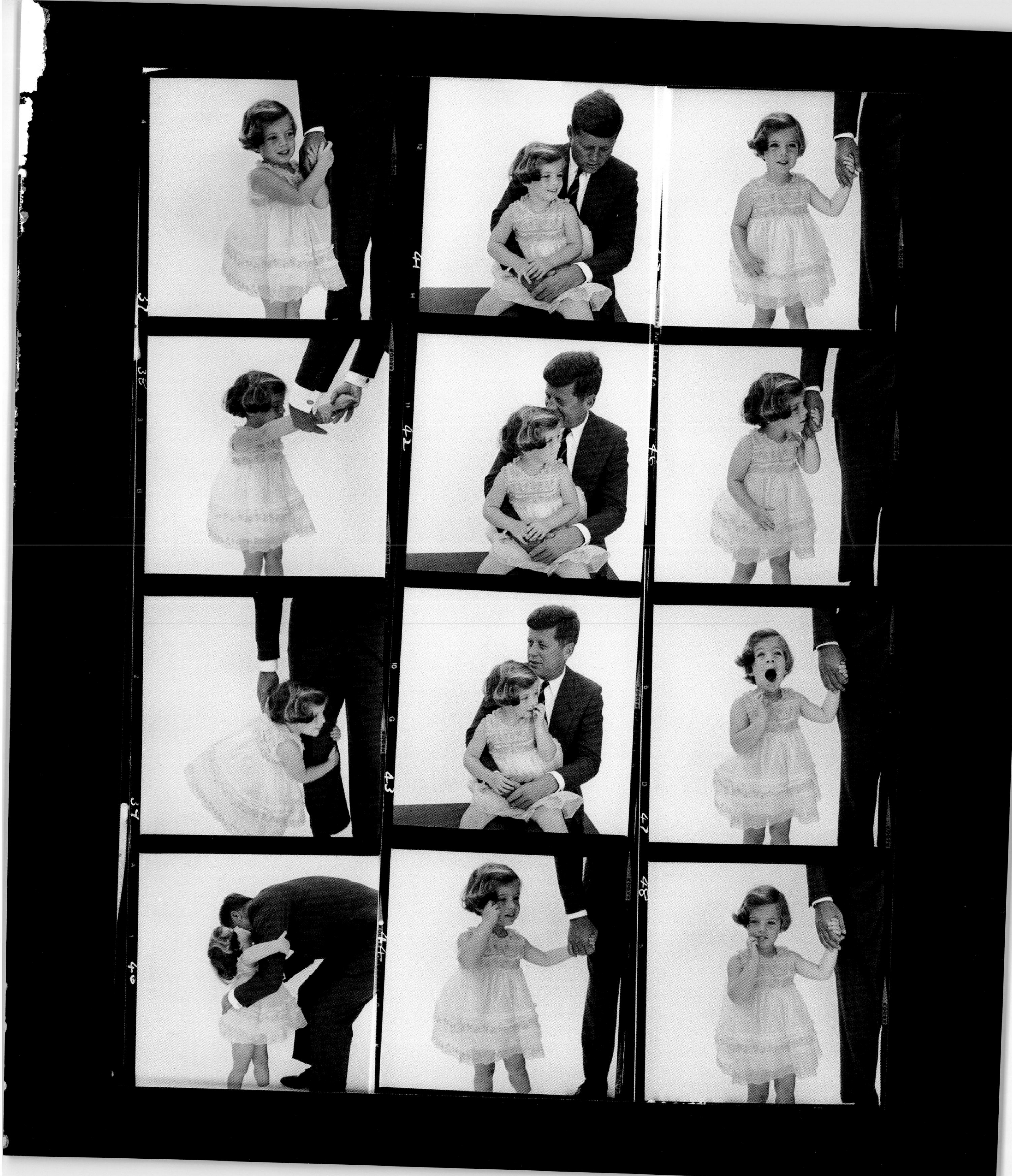

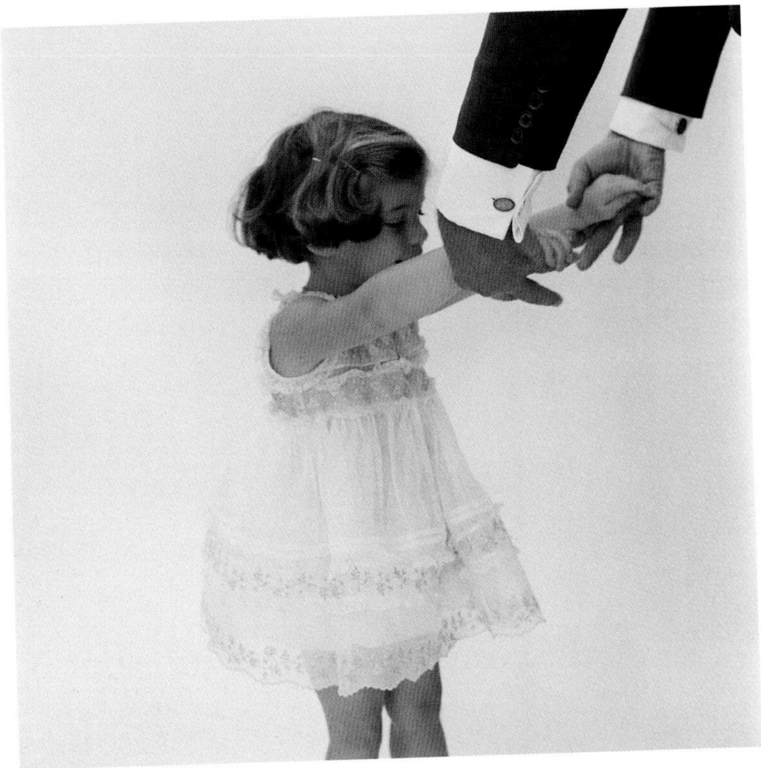

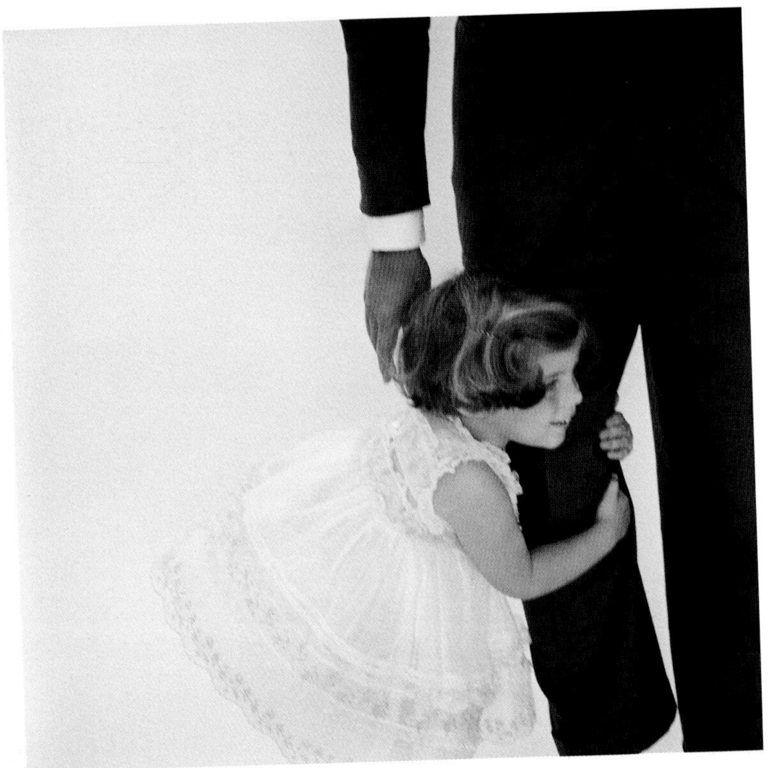

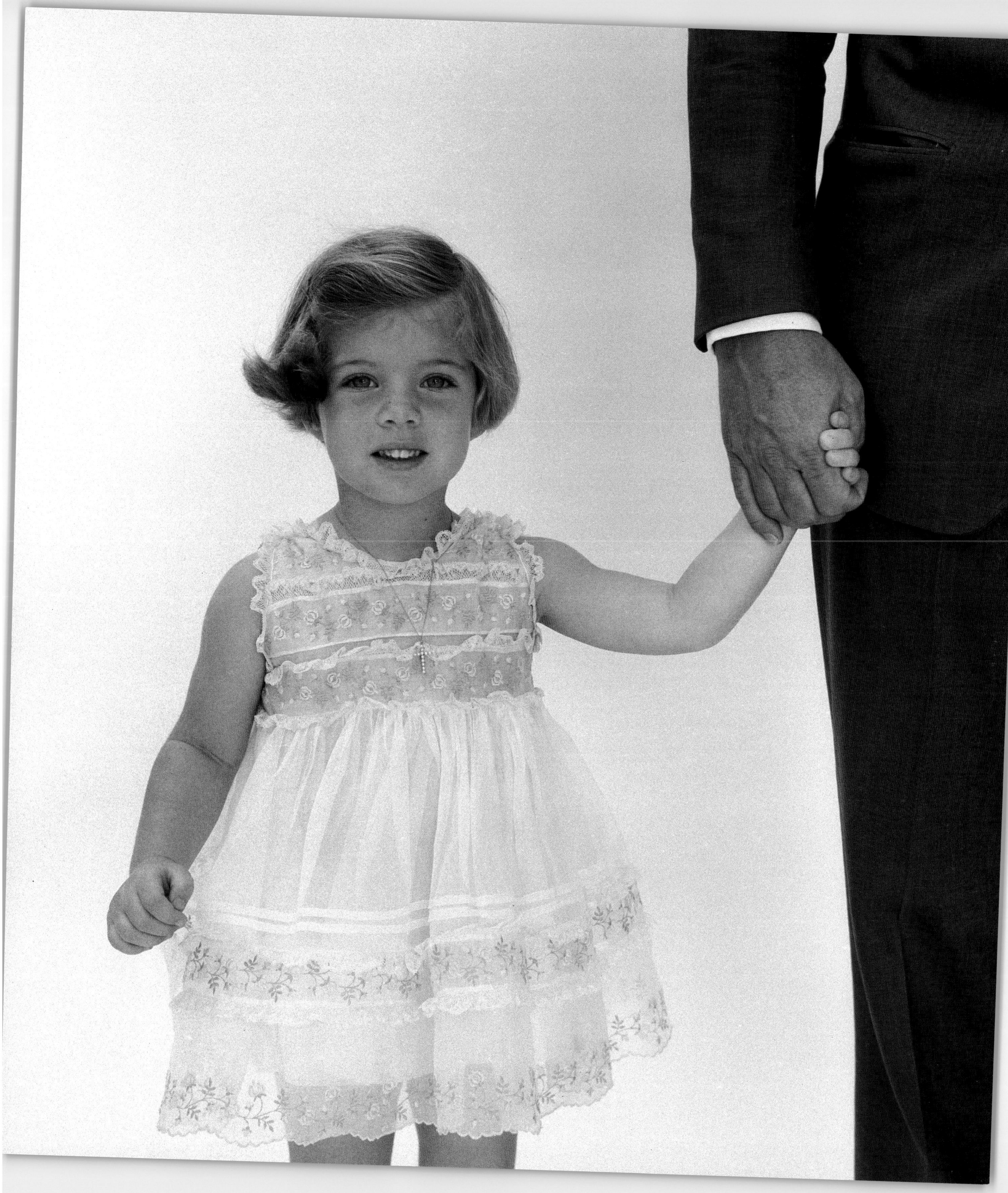

When I wanted President Kennedy to play with Caroline, she stood on his lap while he held her by the knees and she leaned way forward and he would say,

"LET'S PRETEND YOU'RE DIVING INTO THE SEA."

—Richard Avedon in "Look at the Birdie," *Newsweek*, February 6, 1961

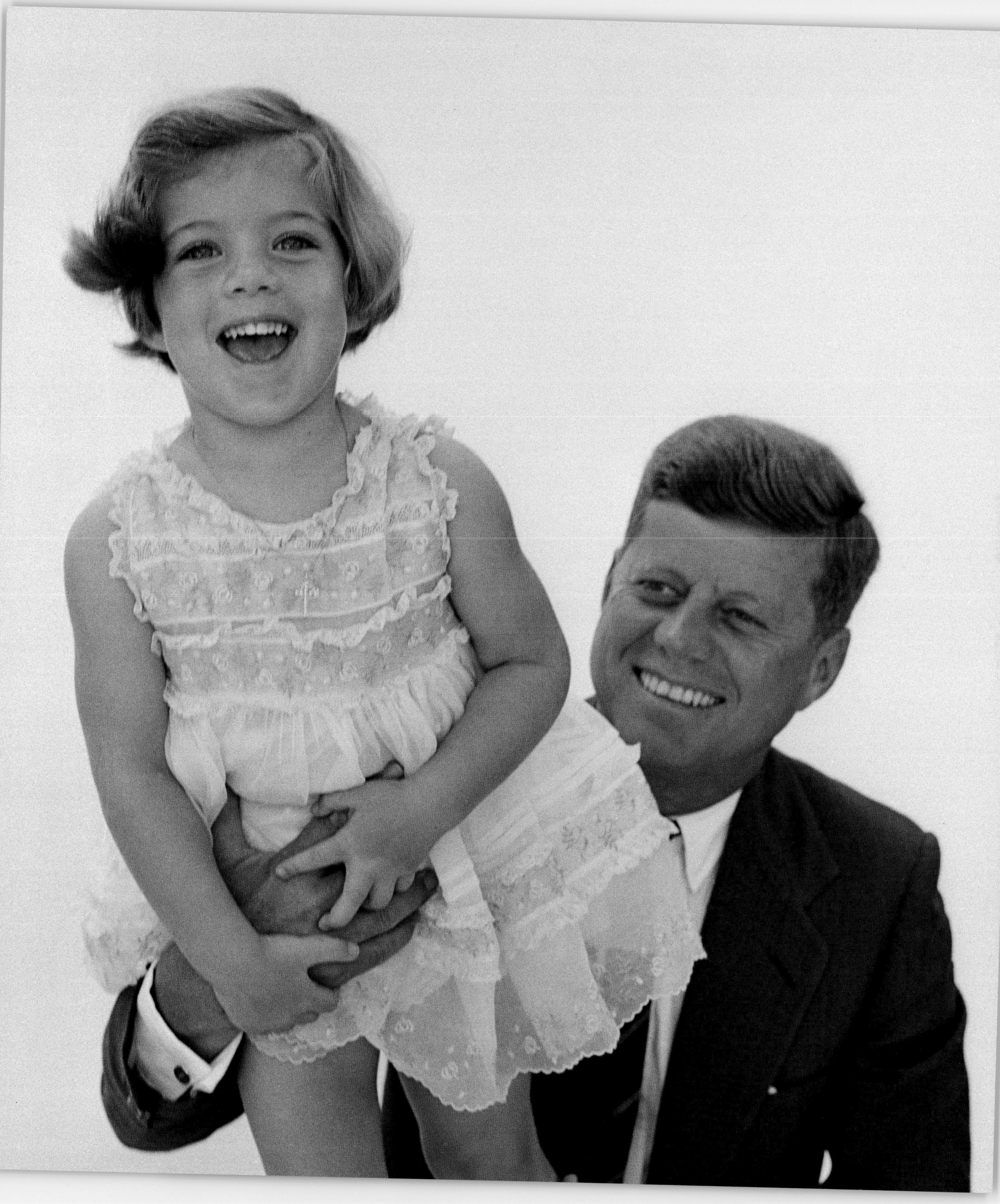

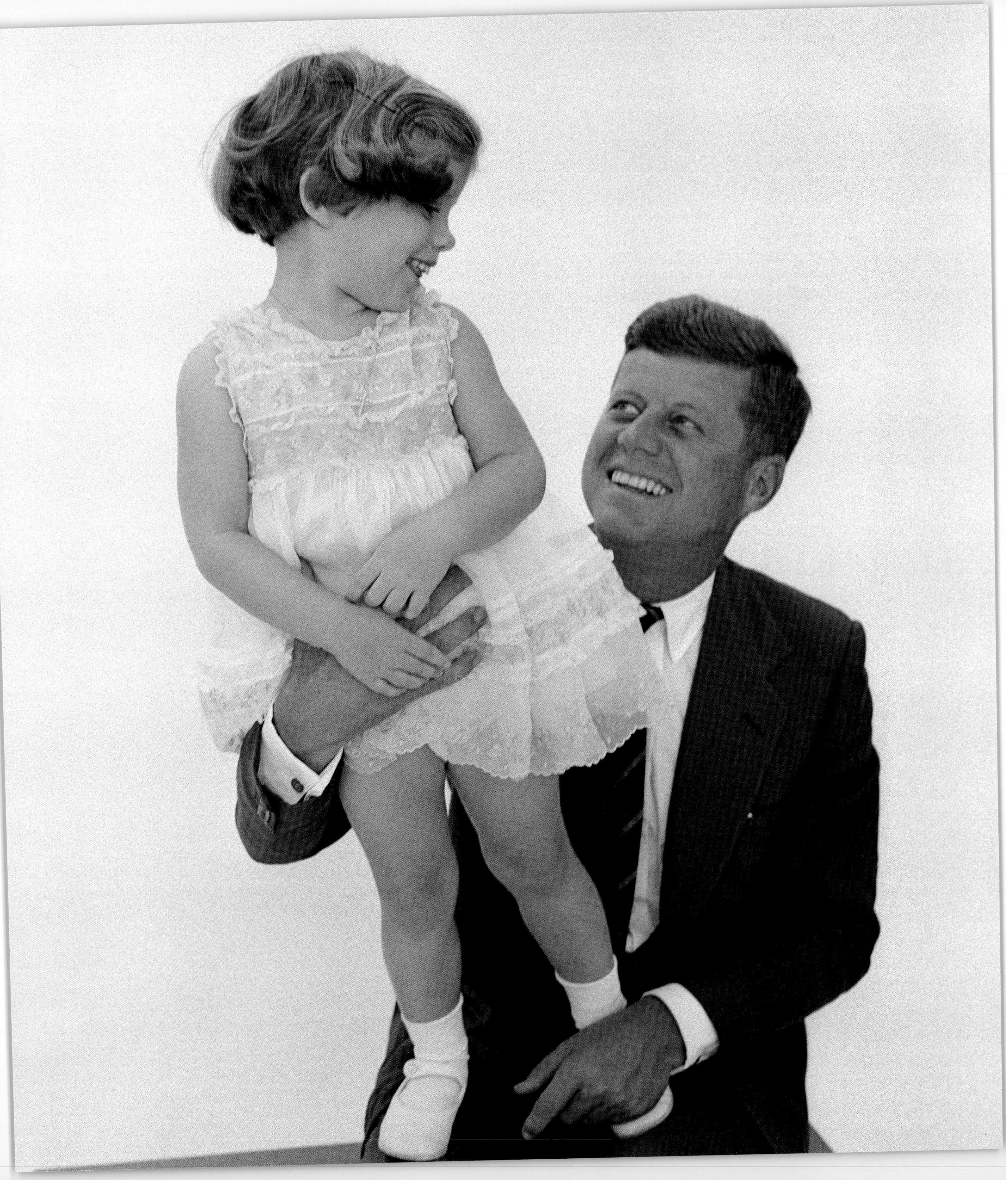

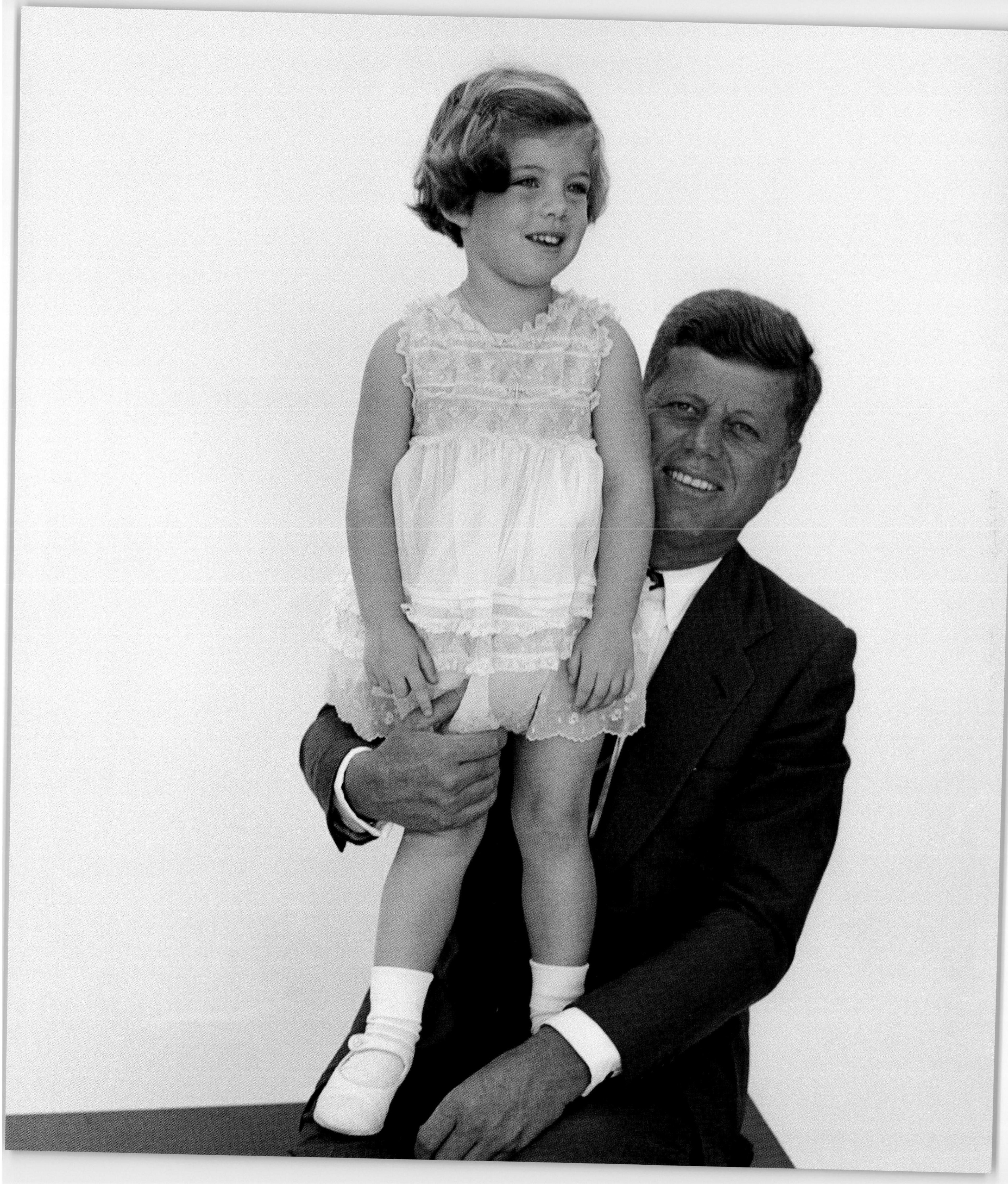

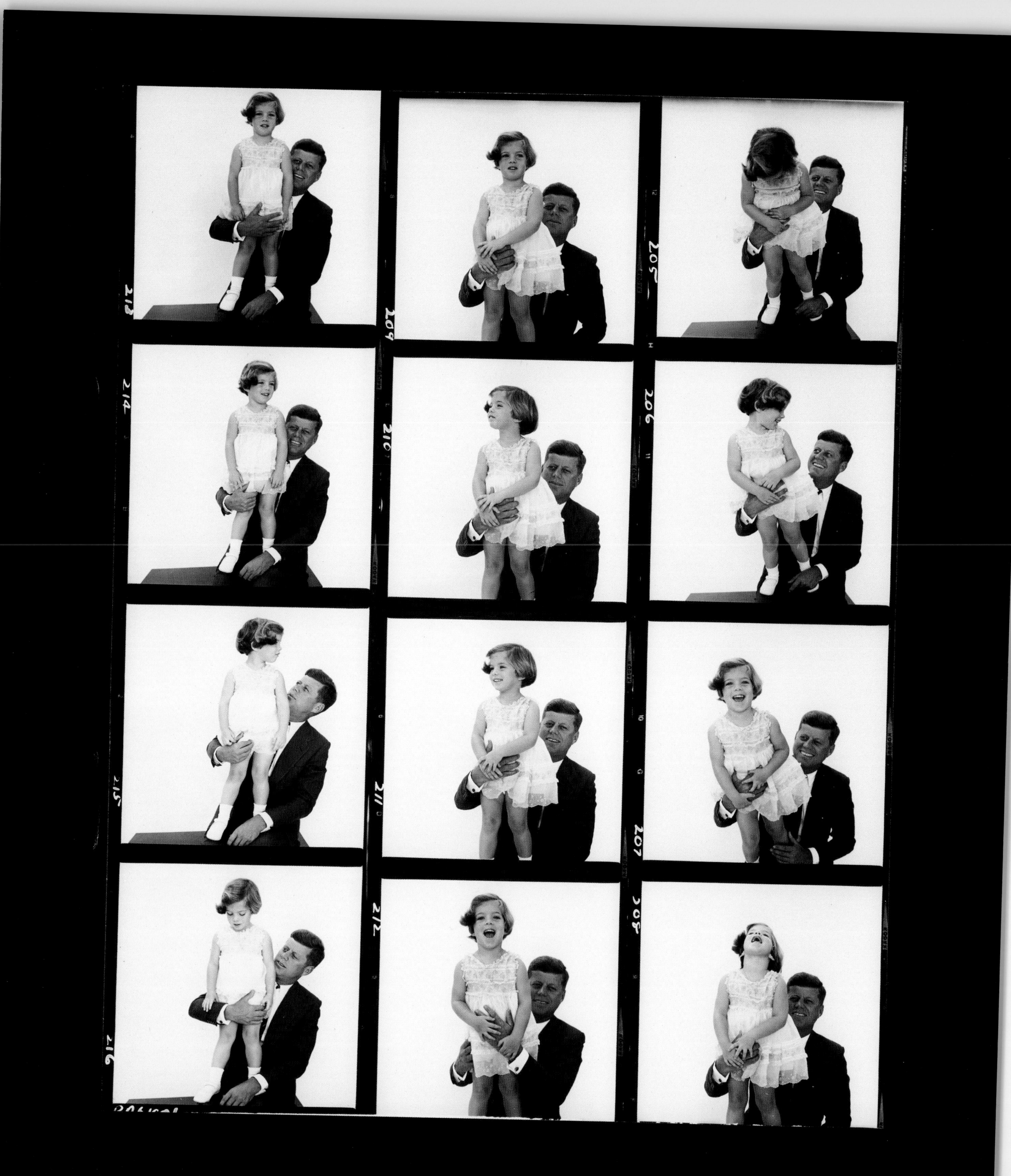

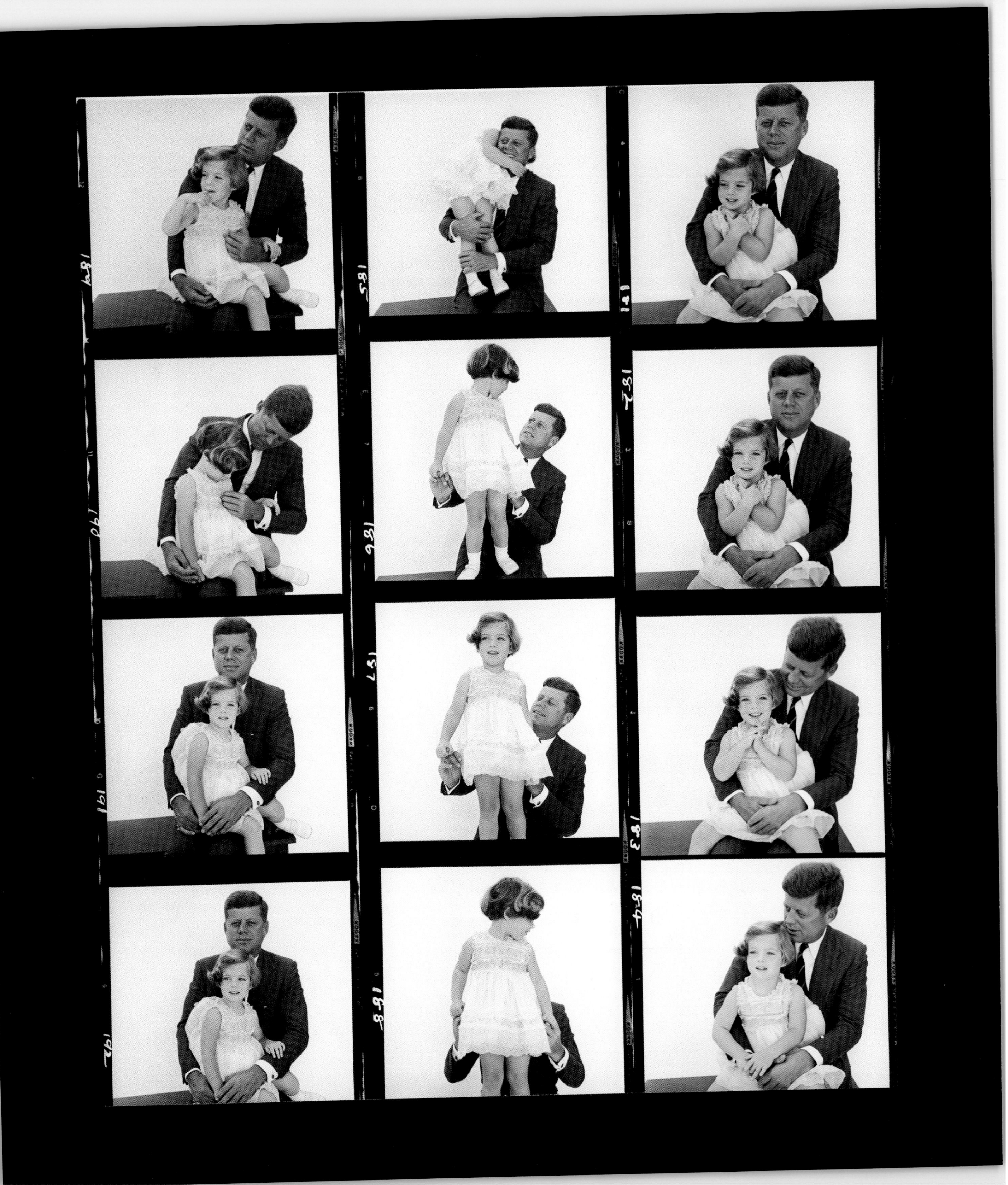
189
185
181
190
186
182
191
187
183
192
188
184

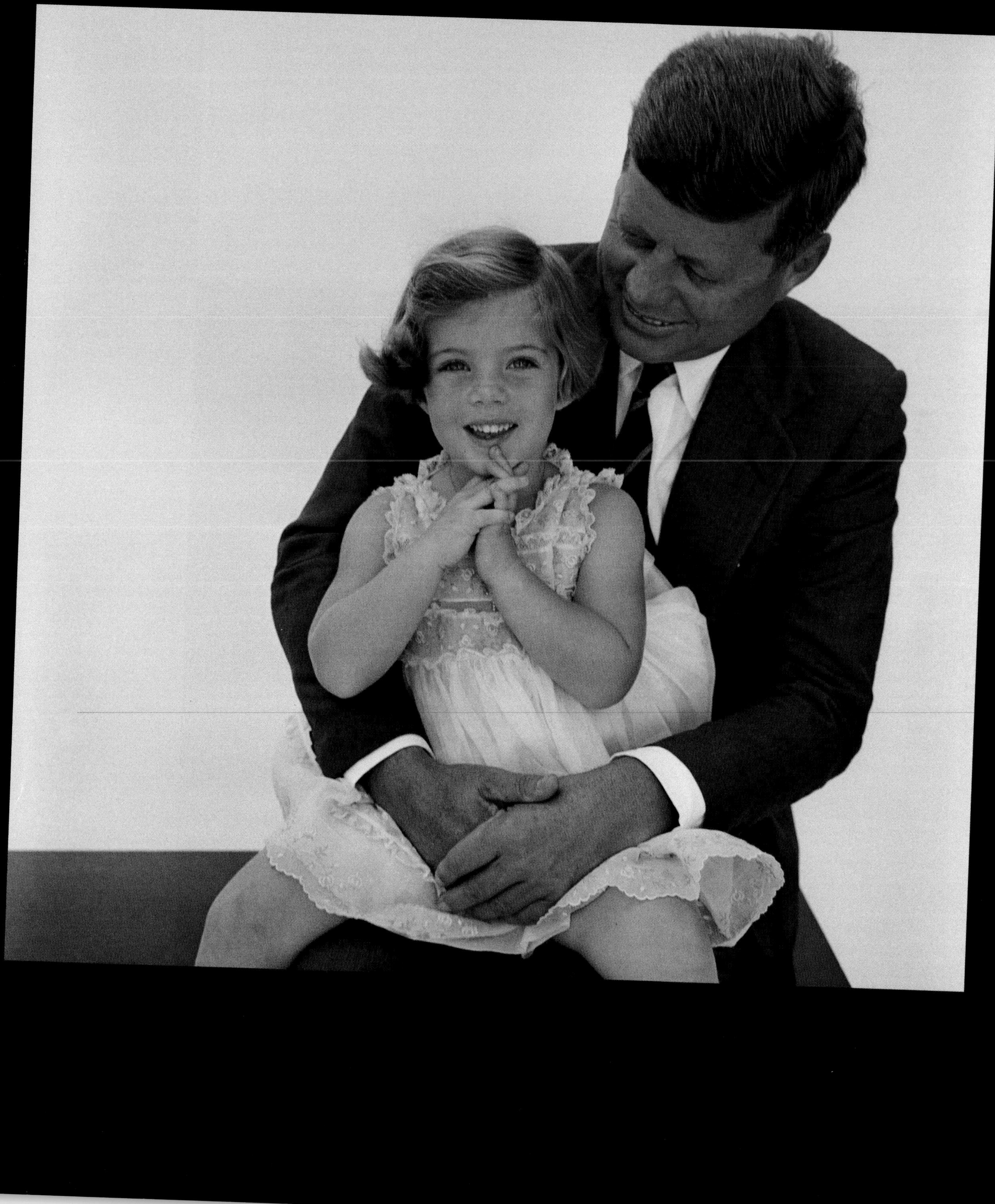

When I took Caroline's picture with her father,

he was dictating memos to his secretary....

When I'd ask him to look around, he'd stop dictating.

But the moment I finished, he'd start in where he left off.

I'VE NEVER SEEN

SUCH A DISPLAY OF MENTAL CONTROL IN MY LIFE.

—Richard Avedon in "Look at the Birdie," *Newsweek*, February 6, 1961

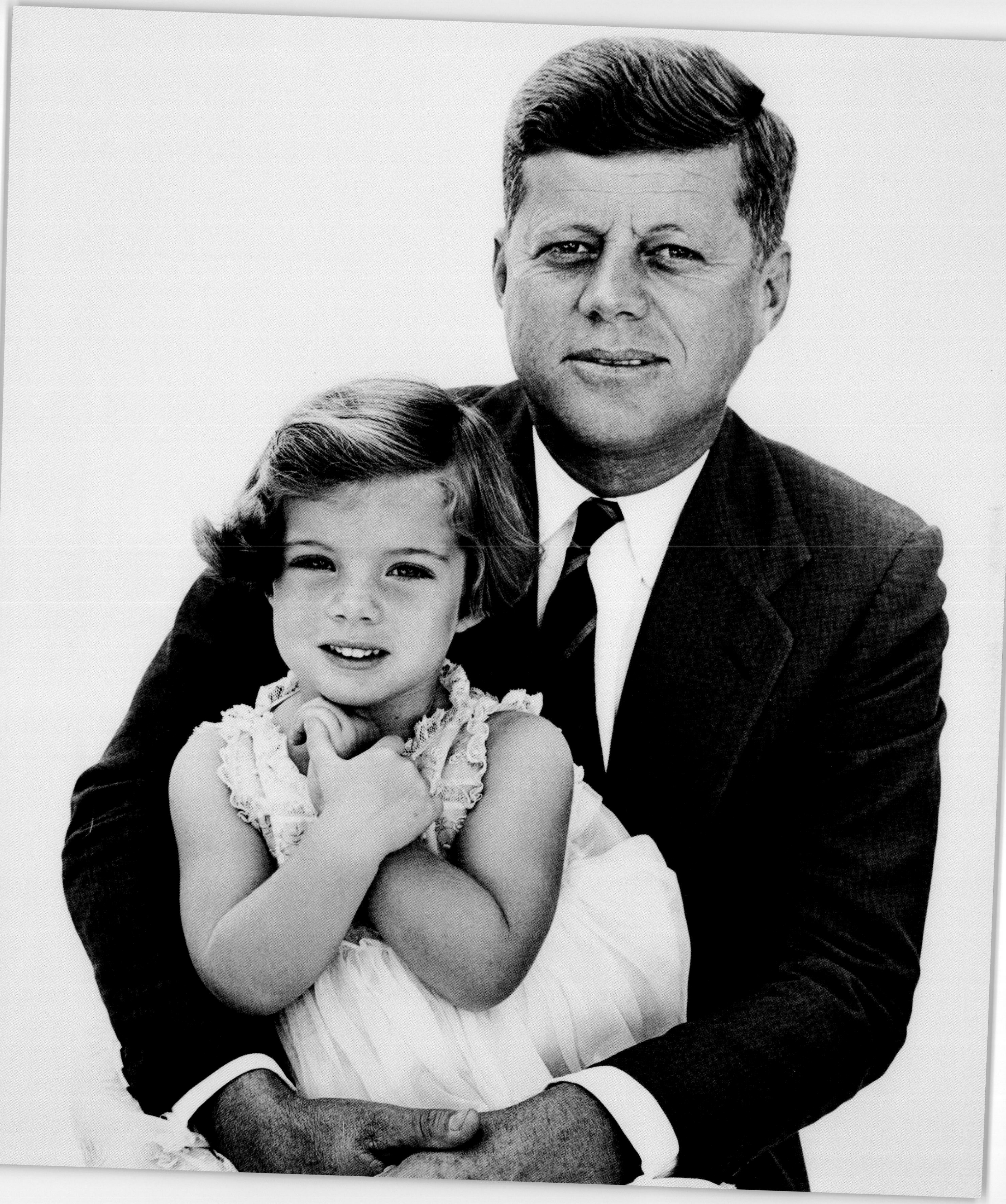

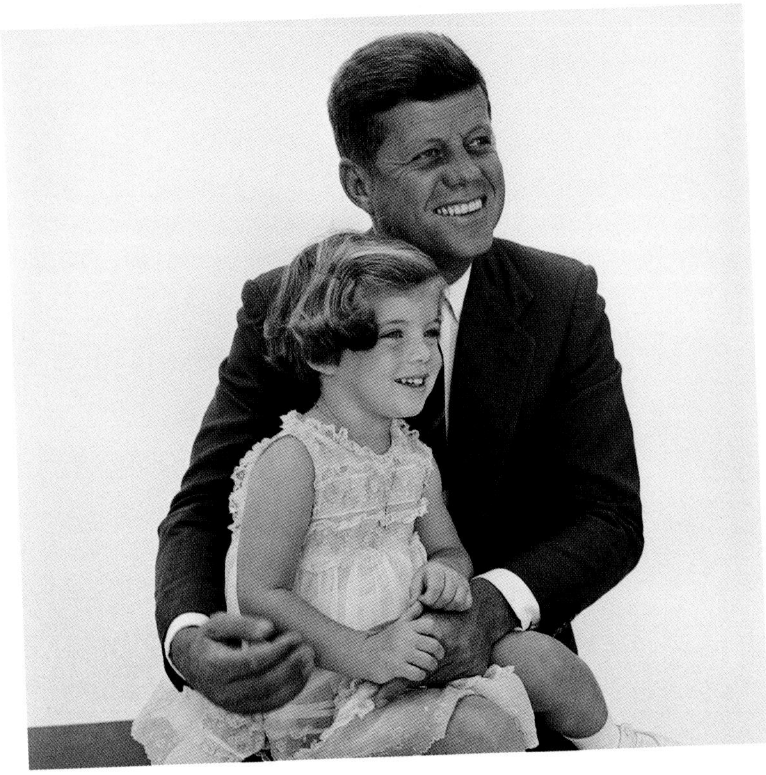

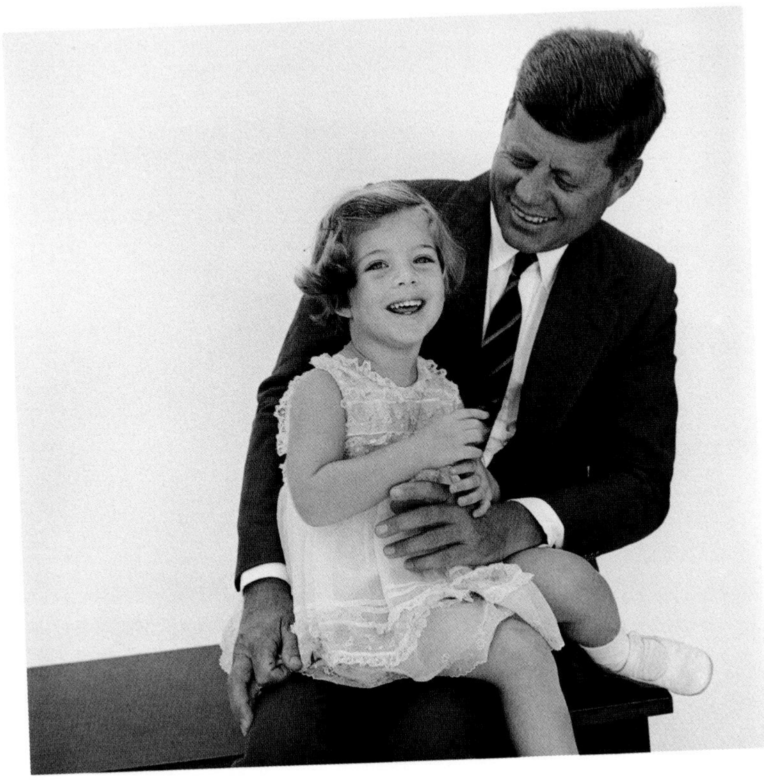

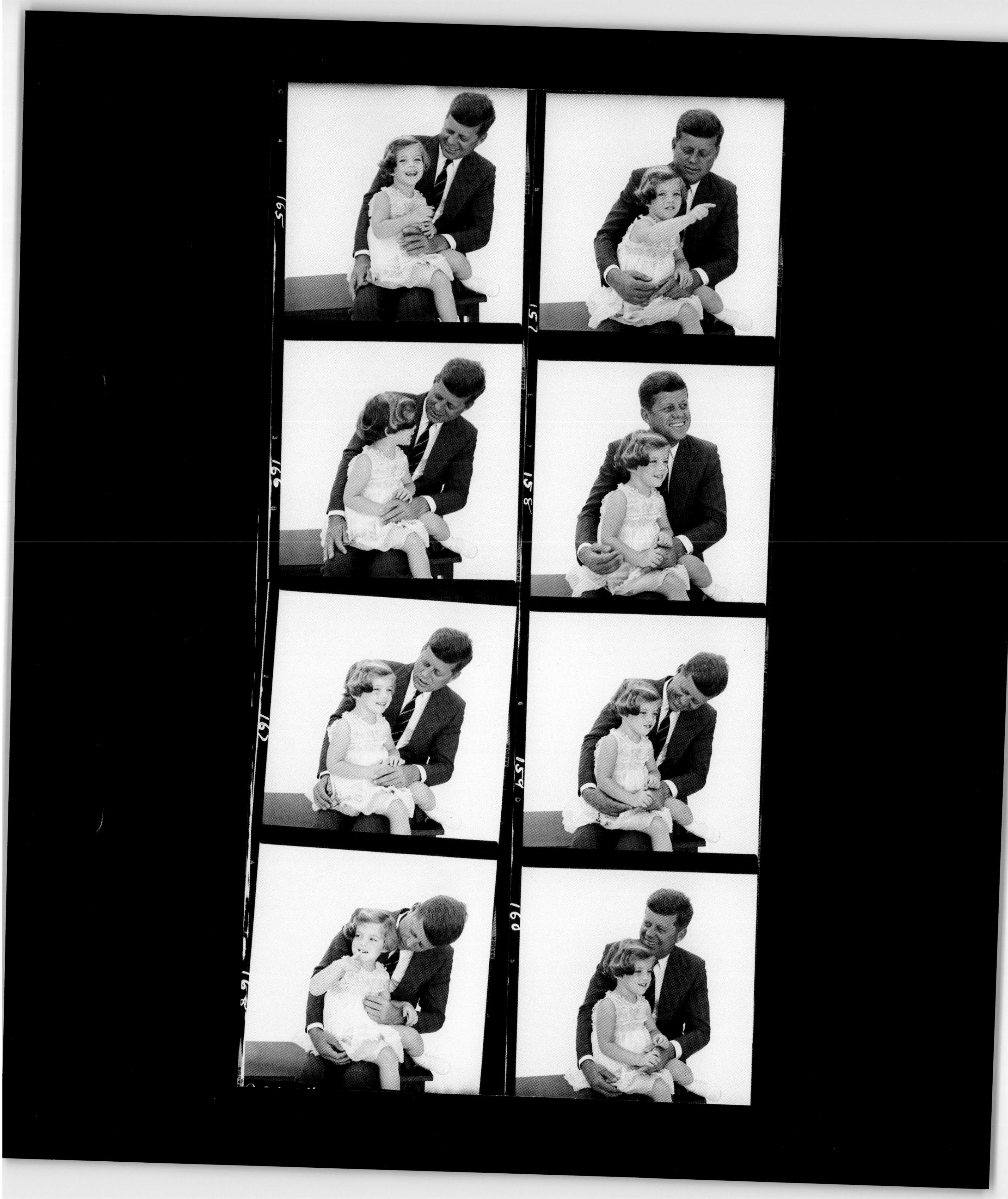

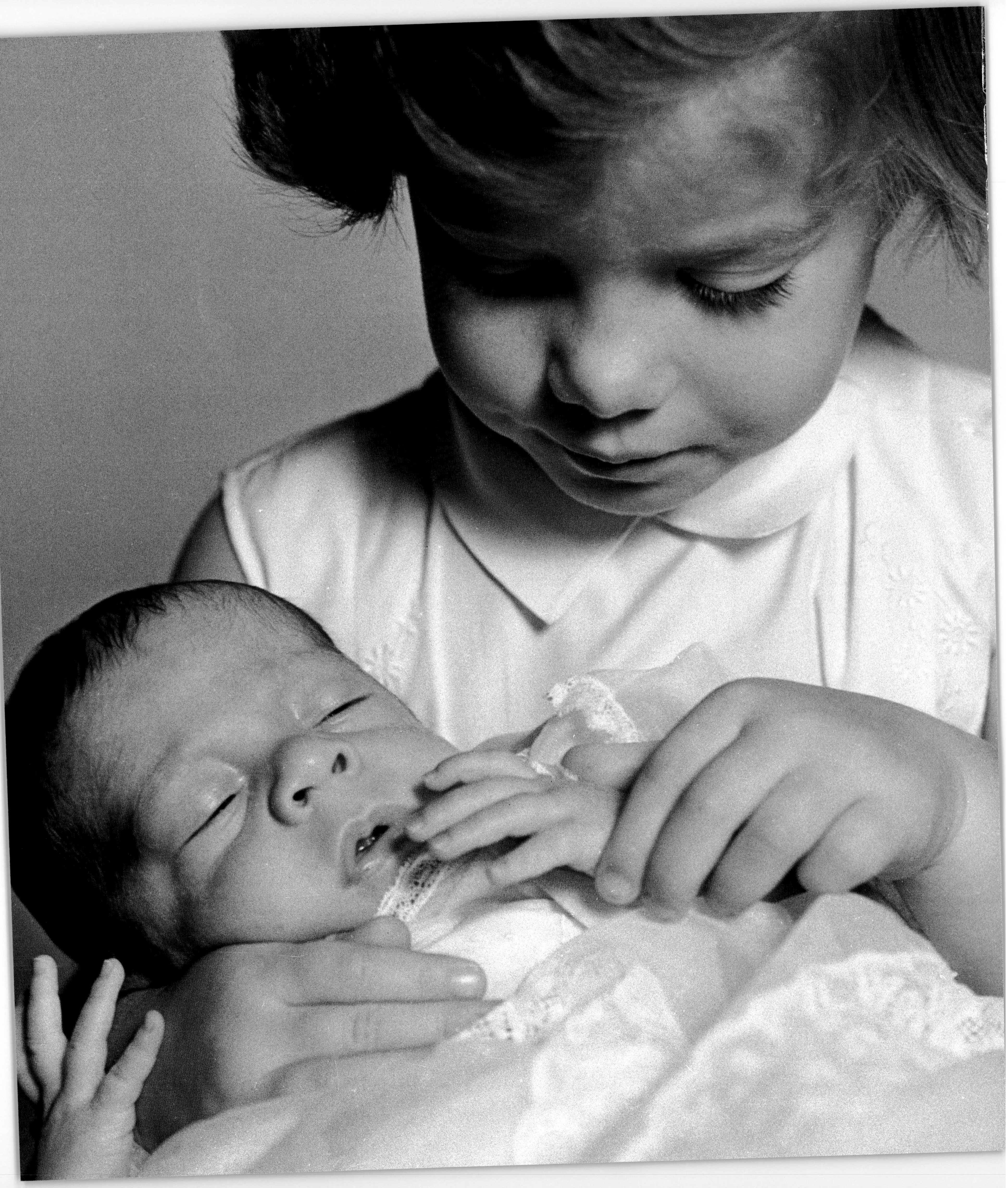

BROTHER AND SISTER

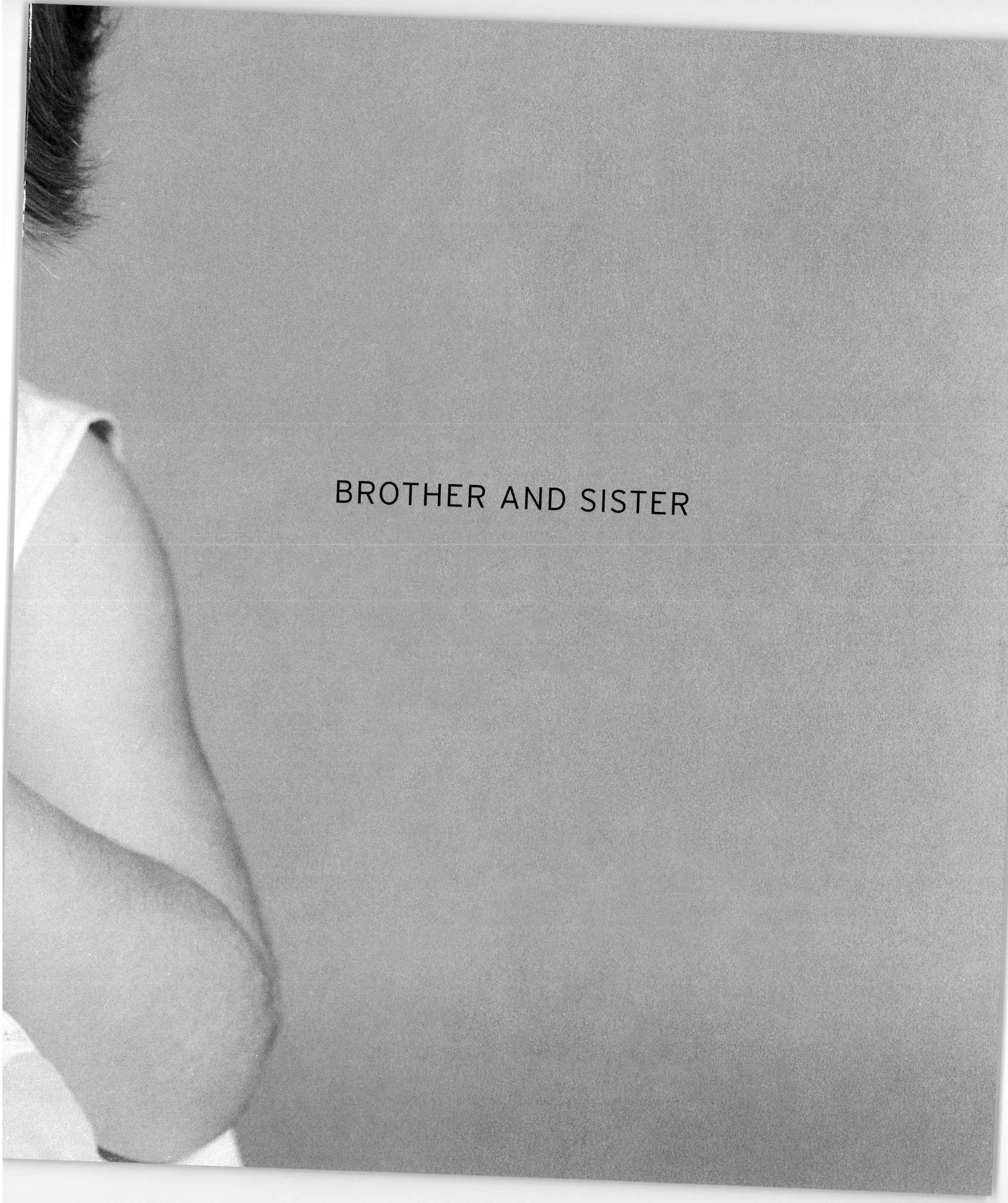

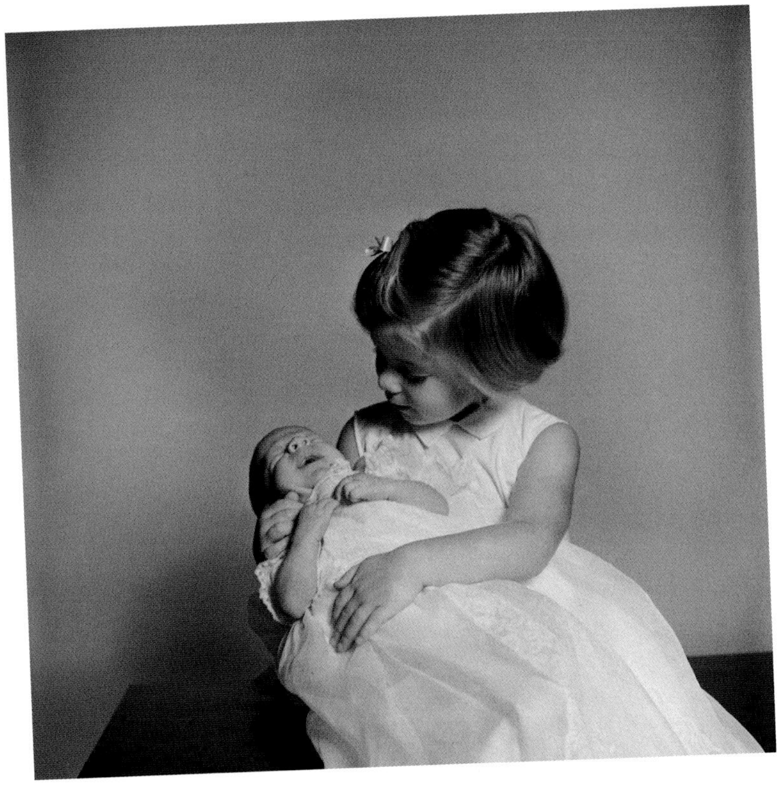

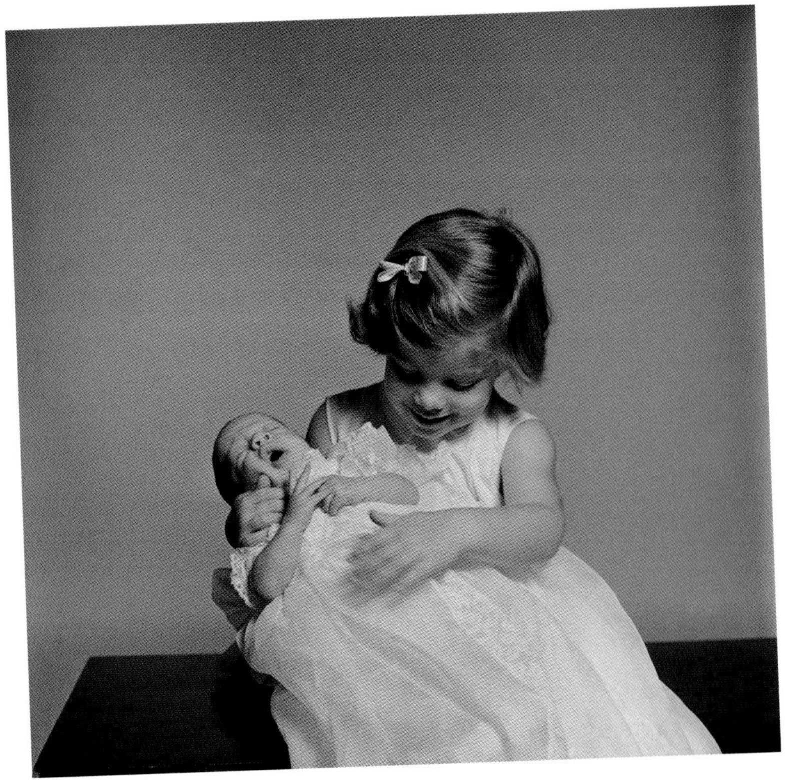

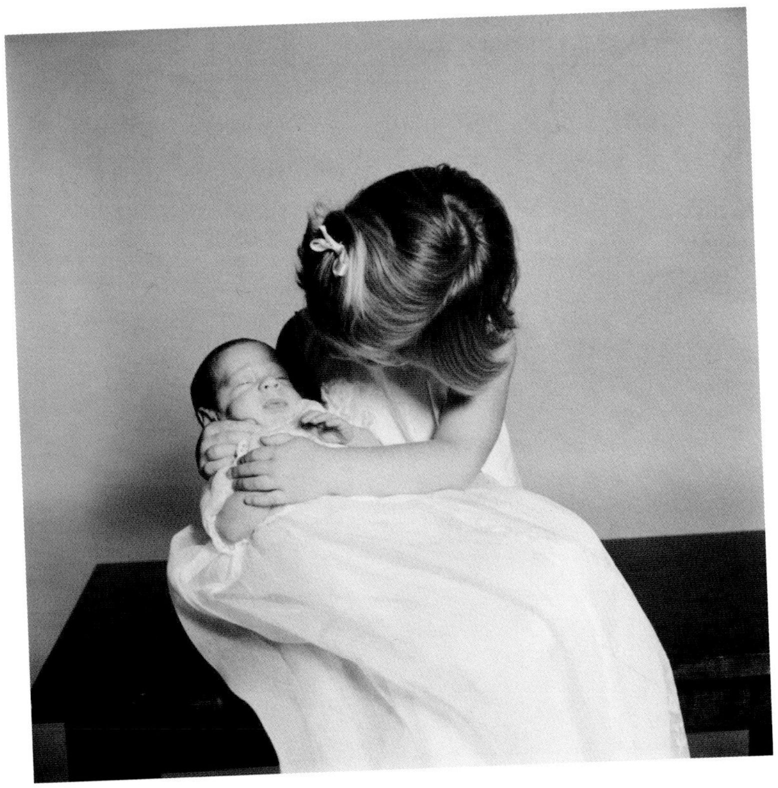

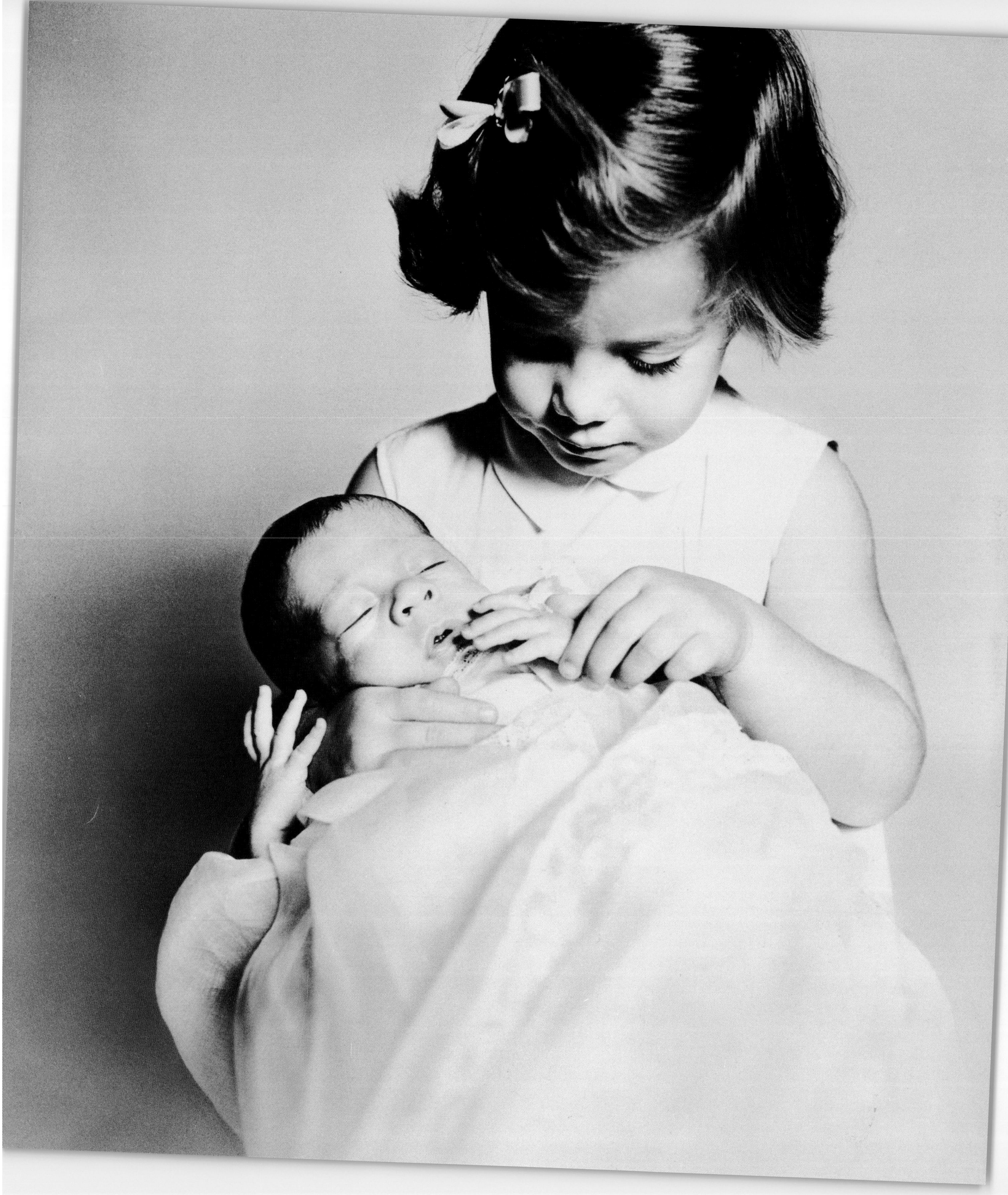

Caroline describes her new brother as

"THE KISSING BABY,"

and when she is permitted to hold him,

she does so responsibly and affectionately.

—*LOOK*, February 28, 1961

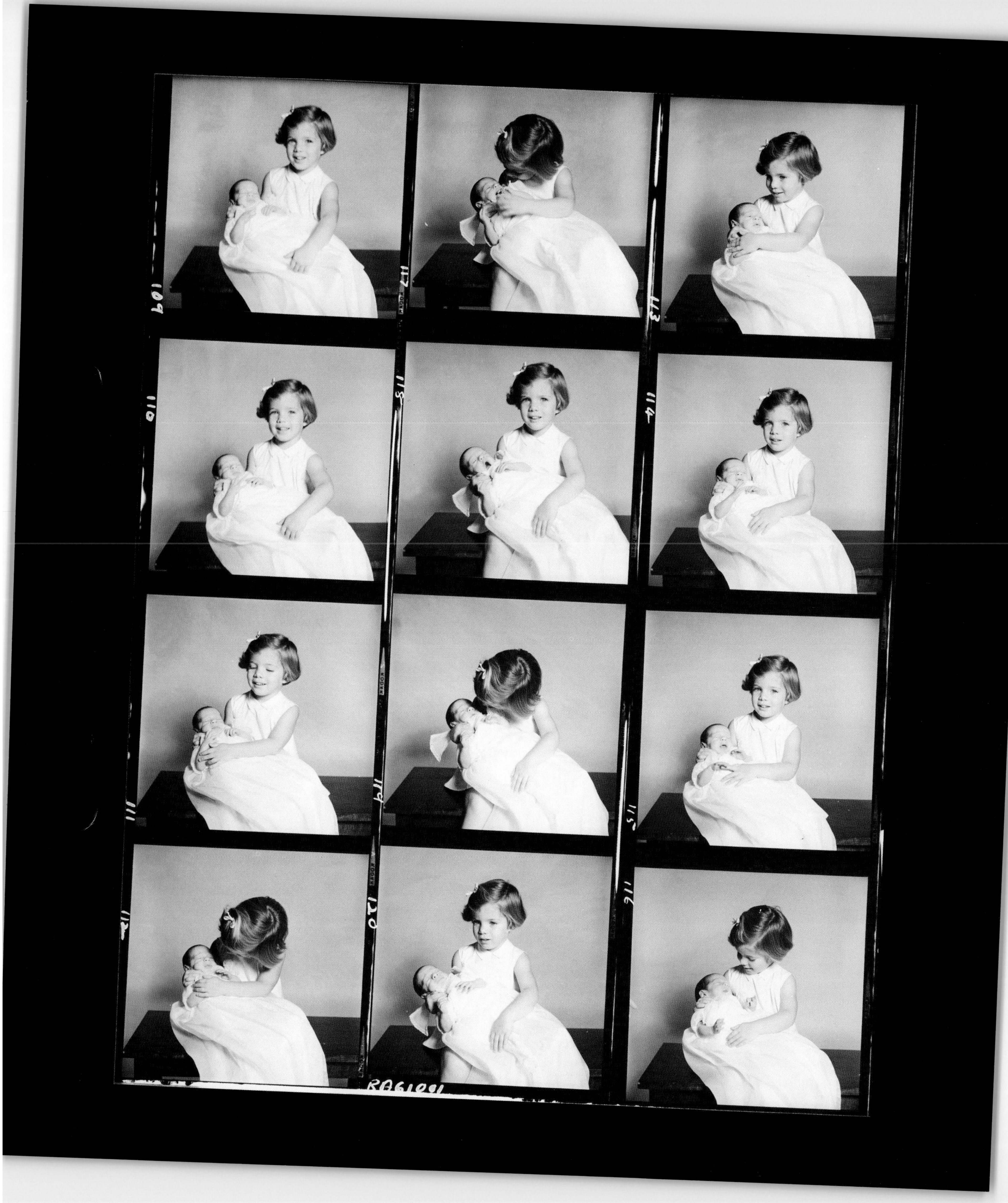
109
117
113
110
118
114
111
119
115
112
120
116
RA61001

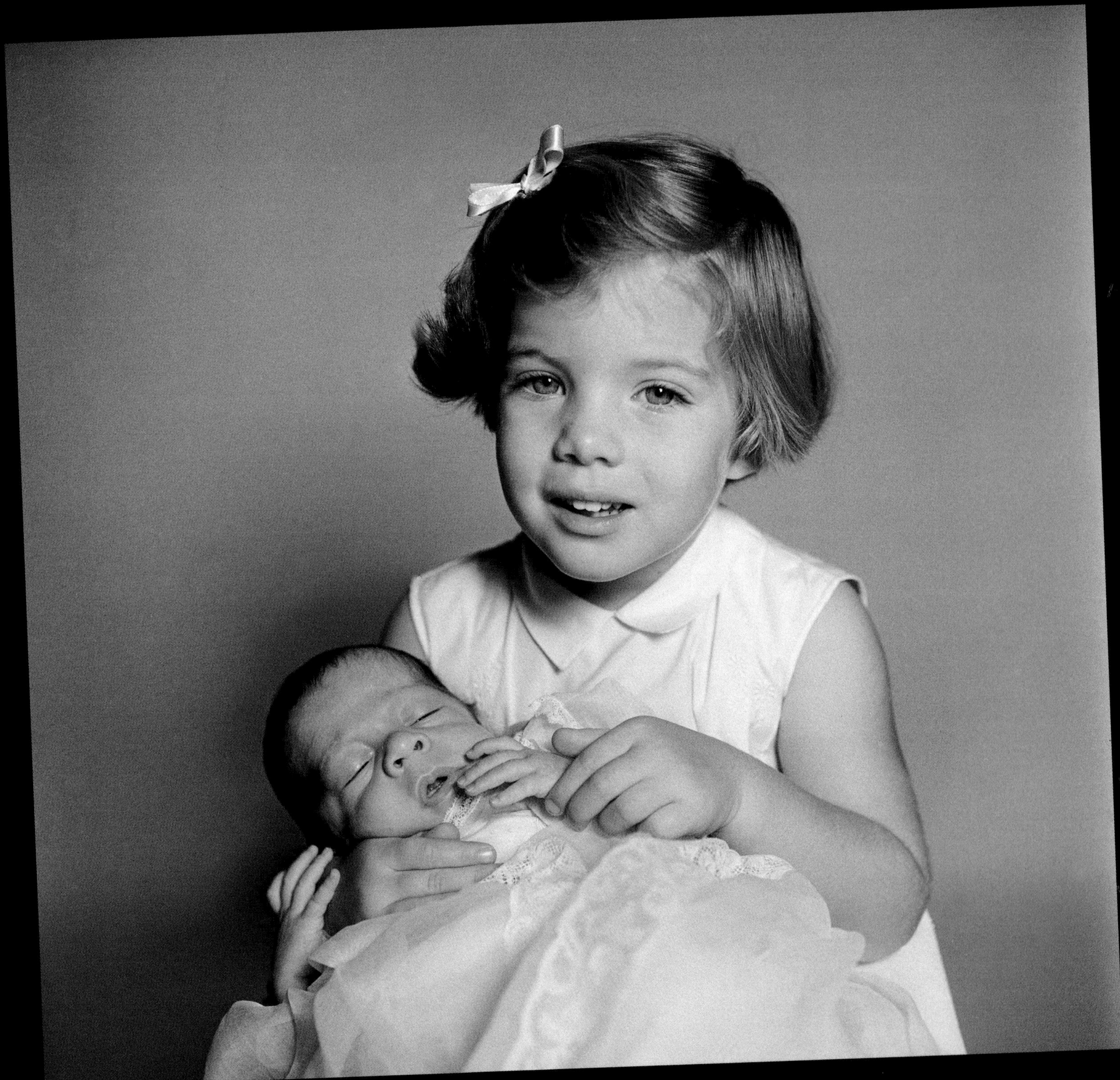

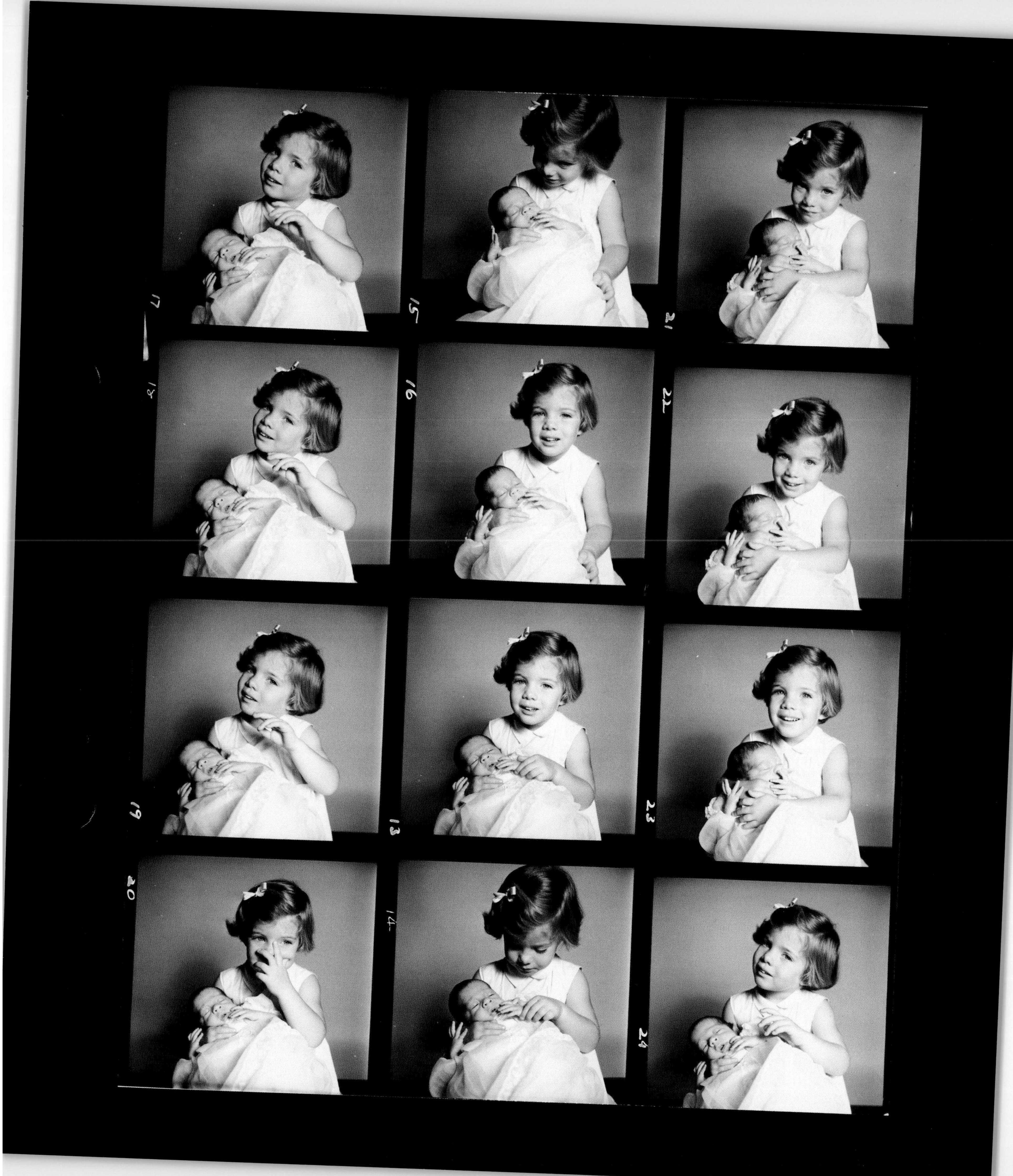

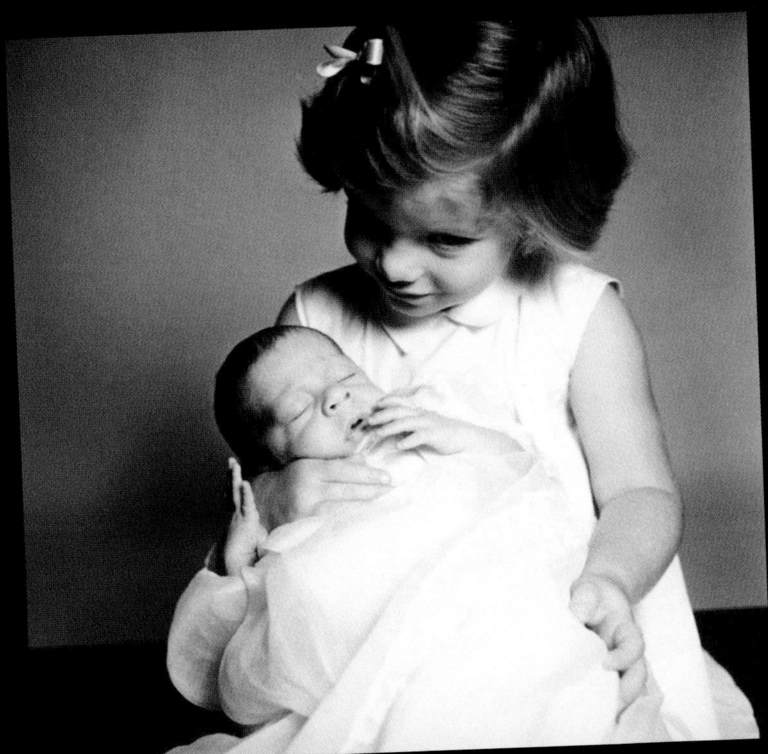

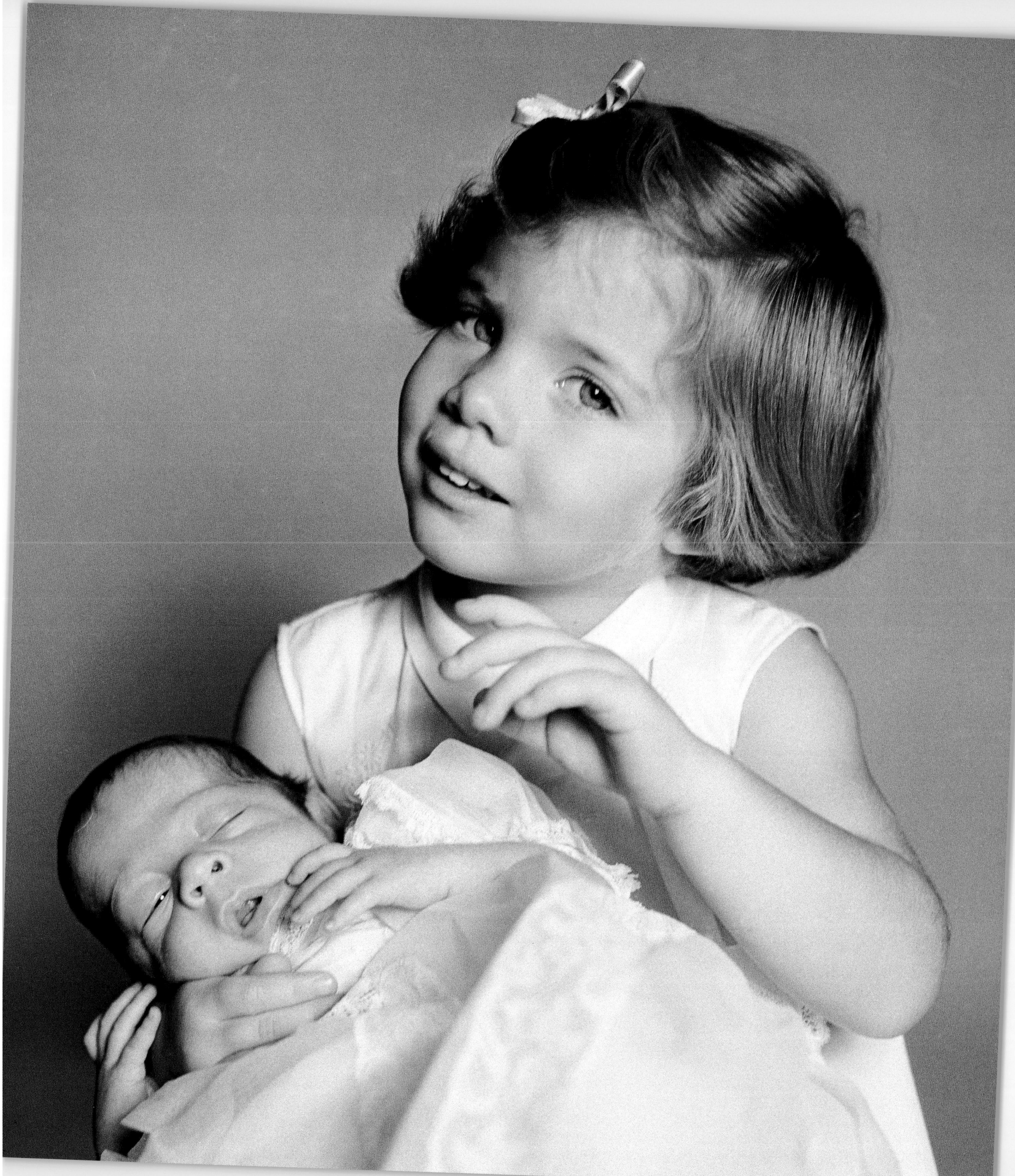

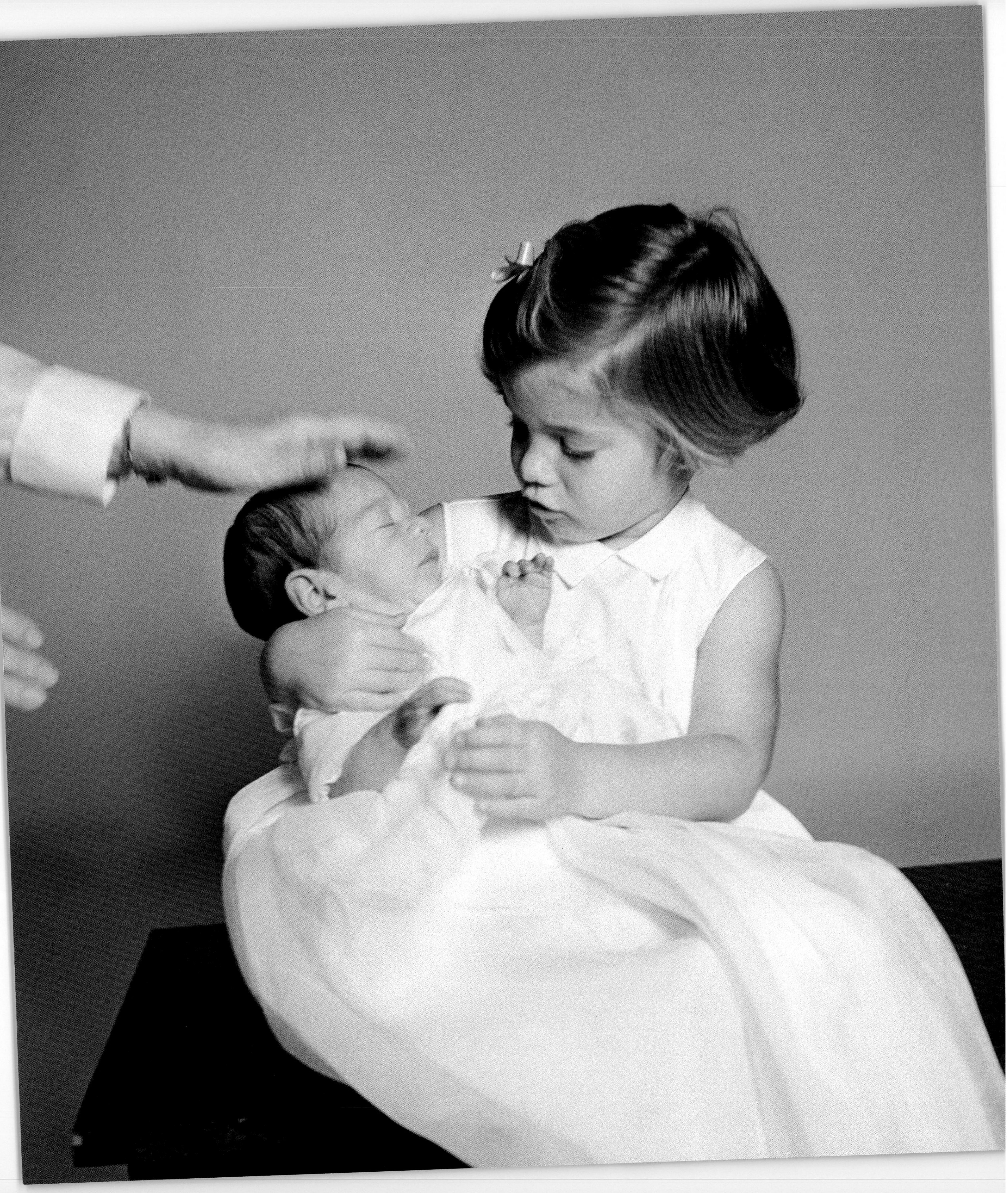

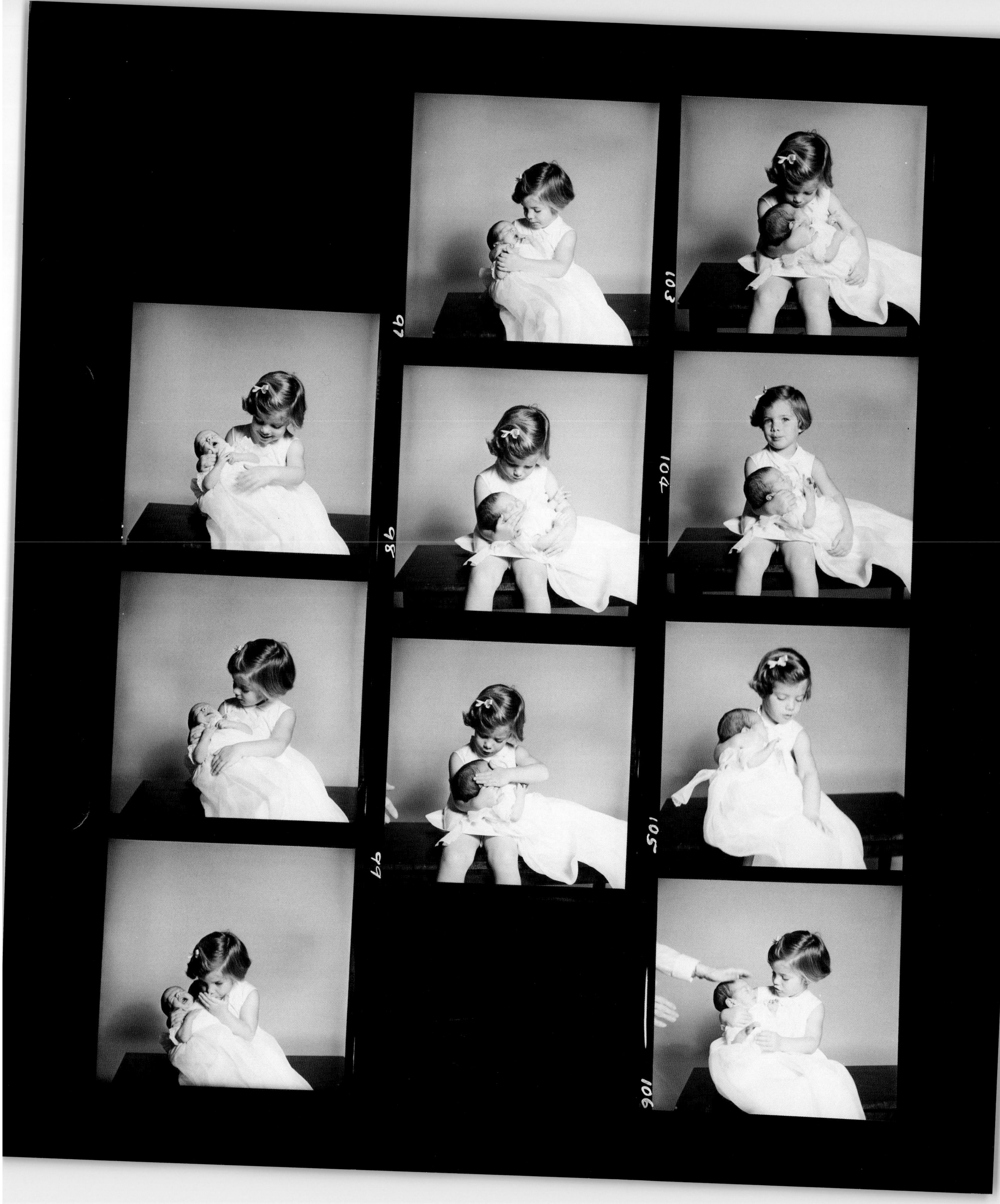
97
103
98
104
99
105
106

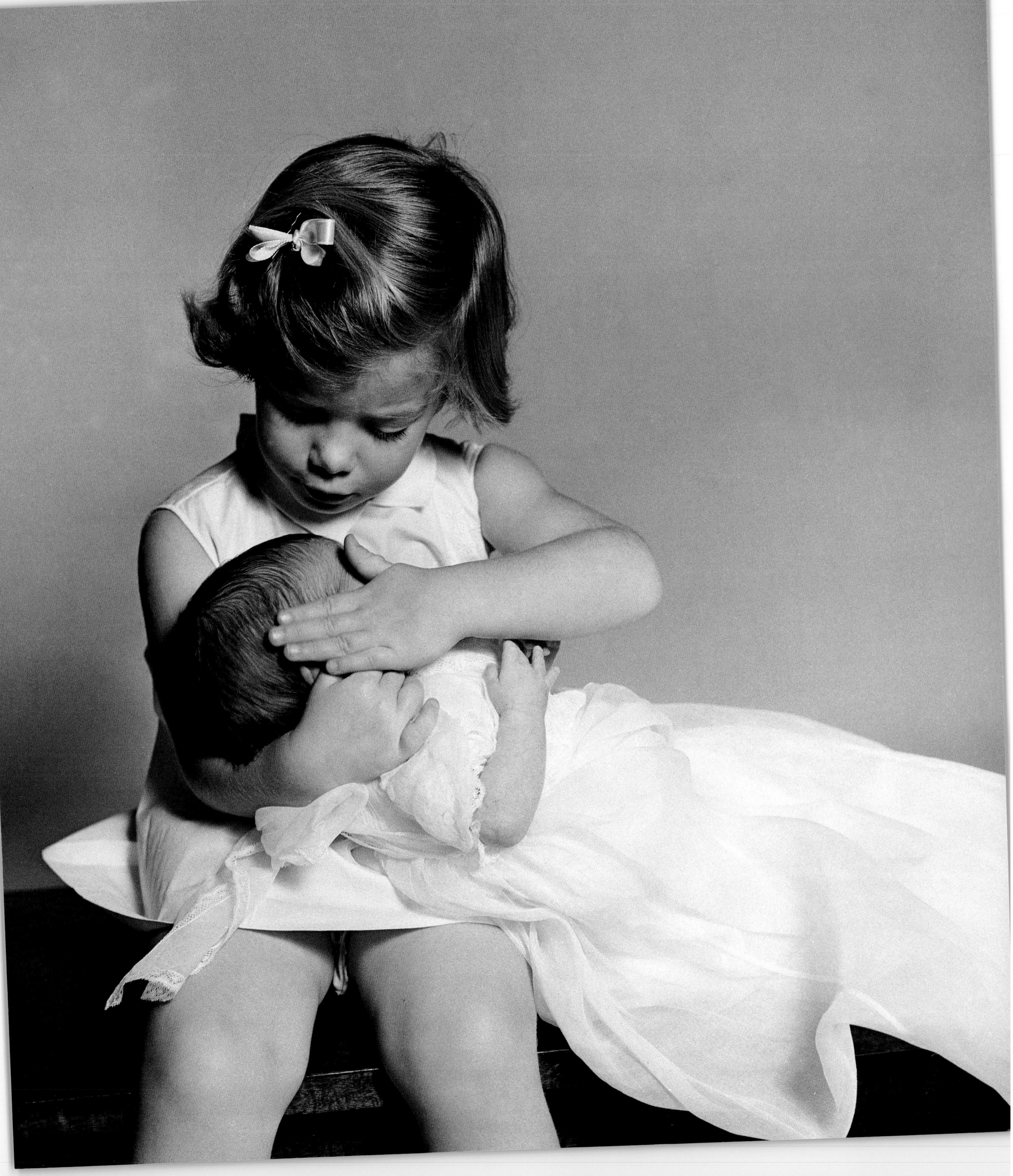

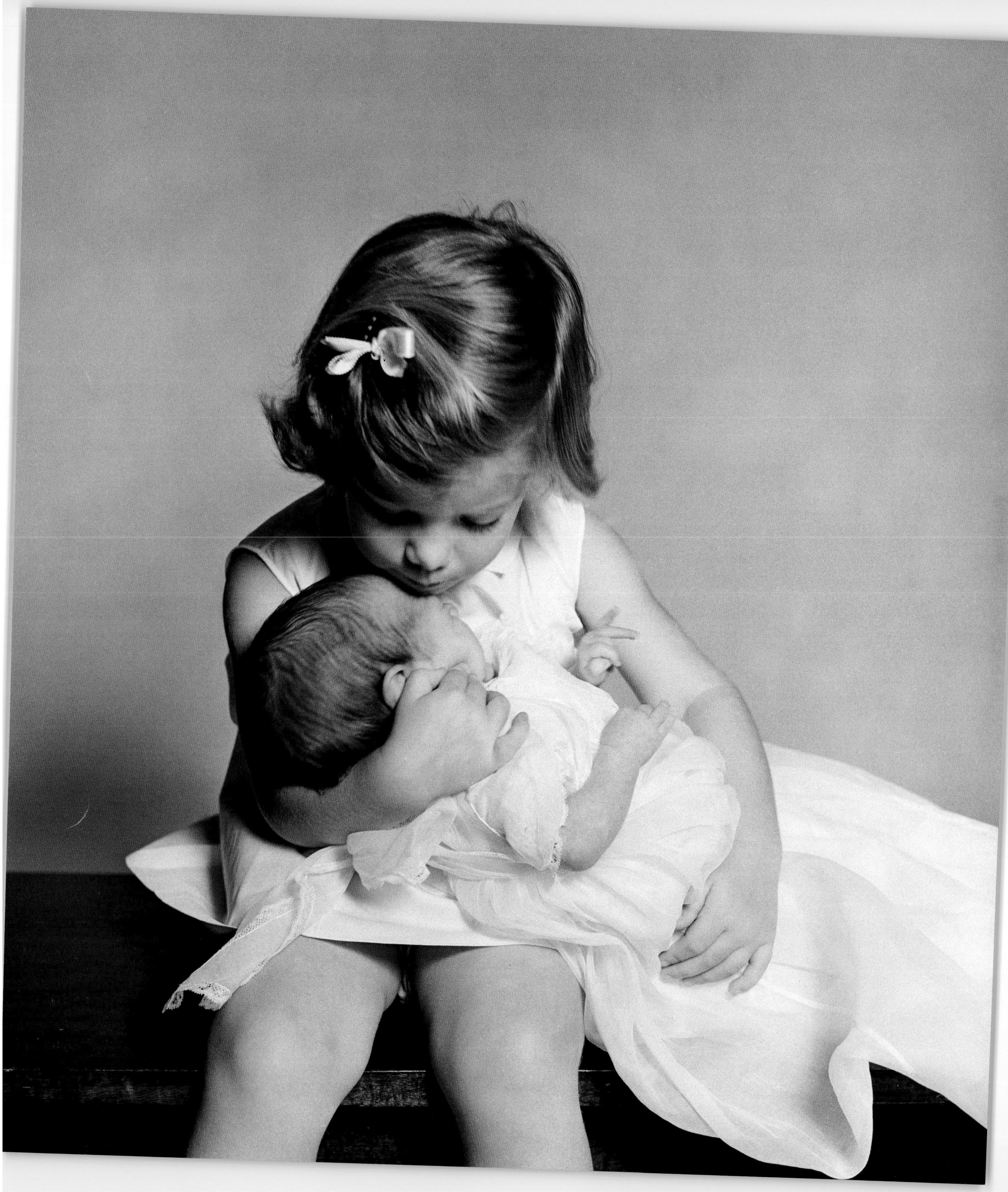

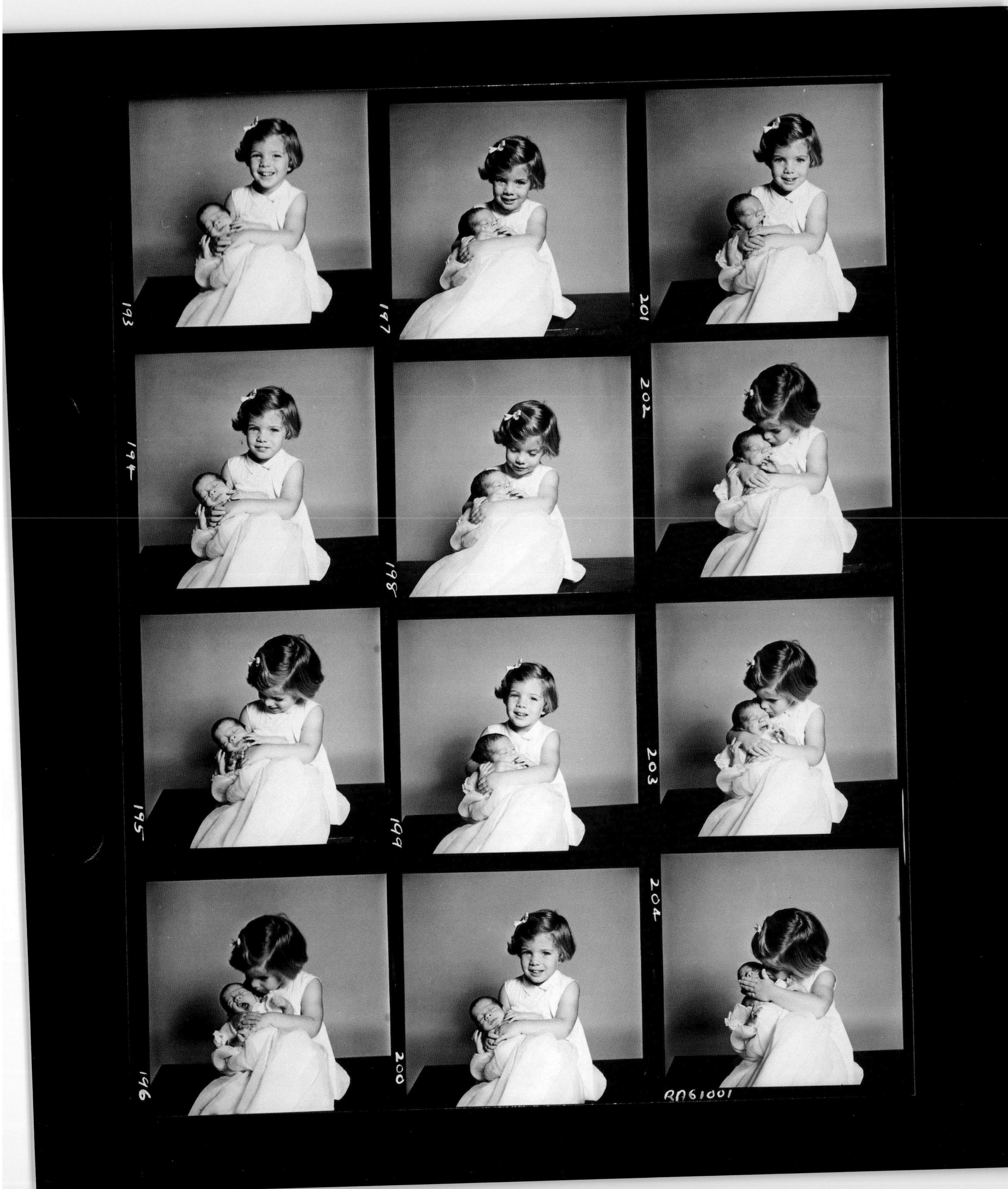

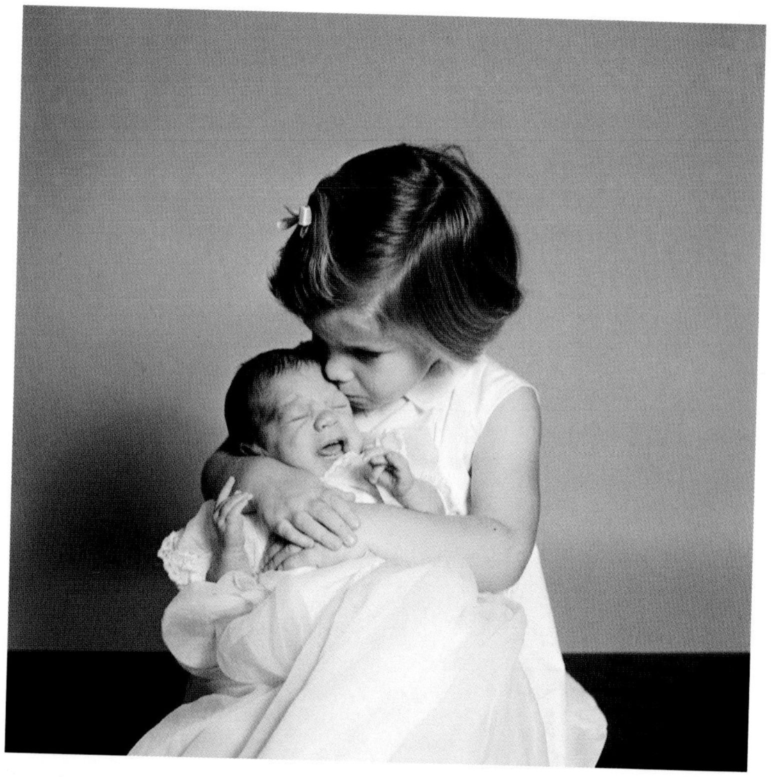

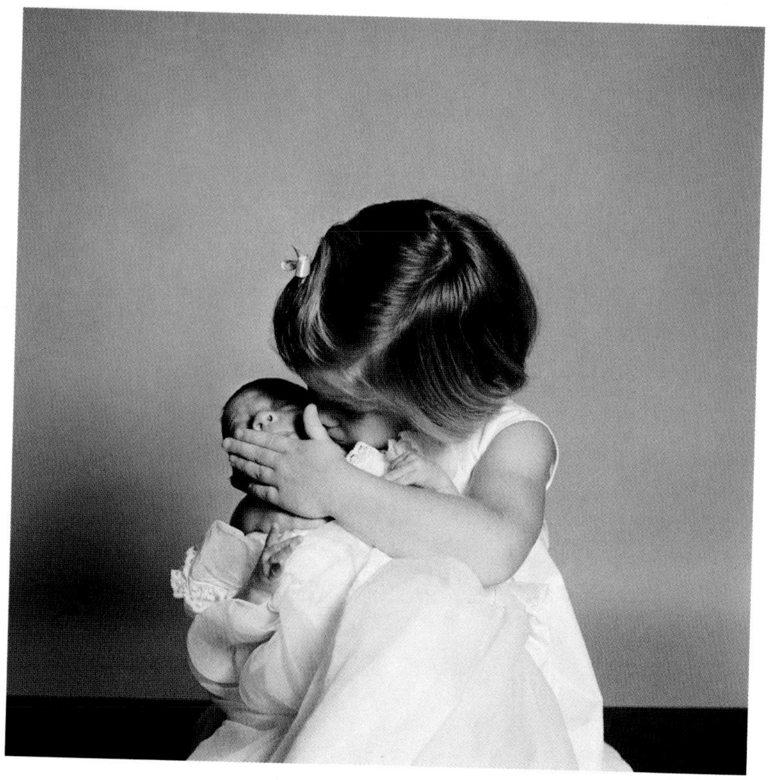

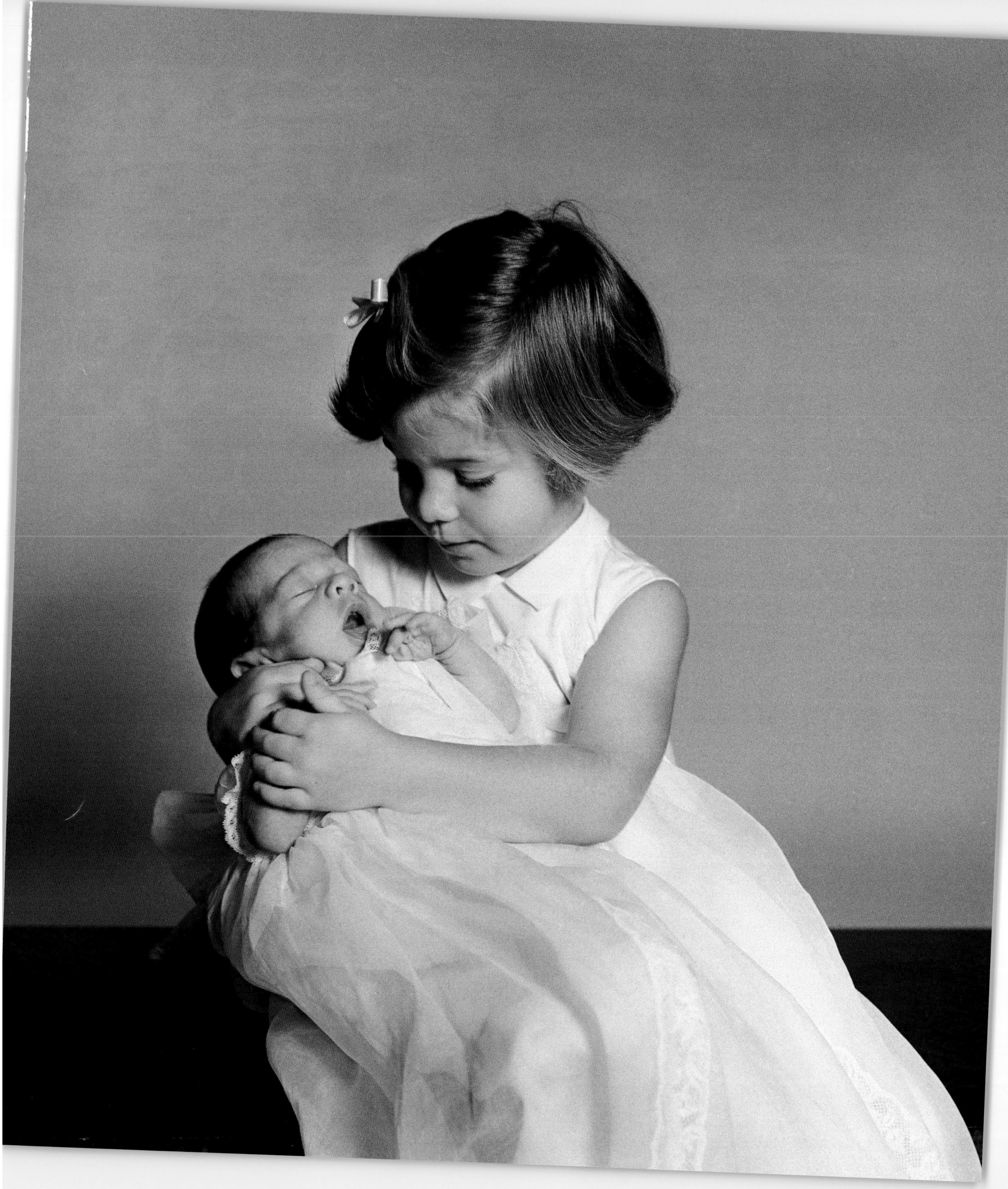

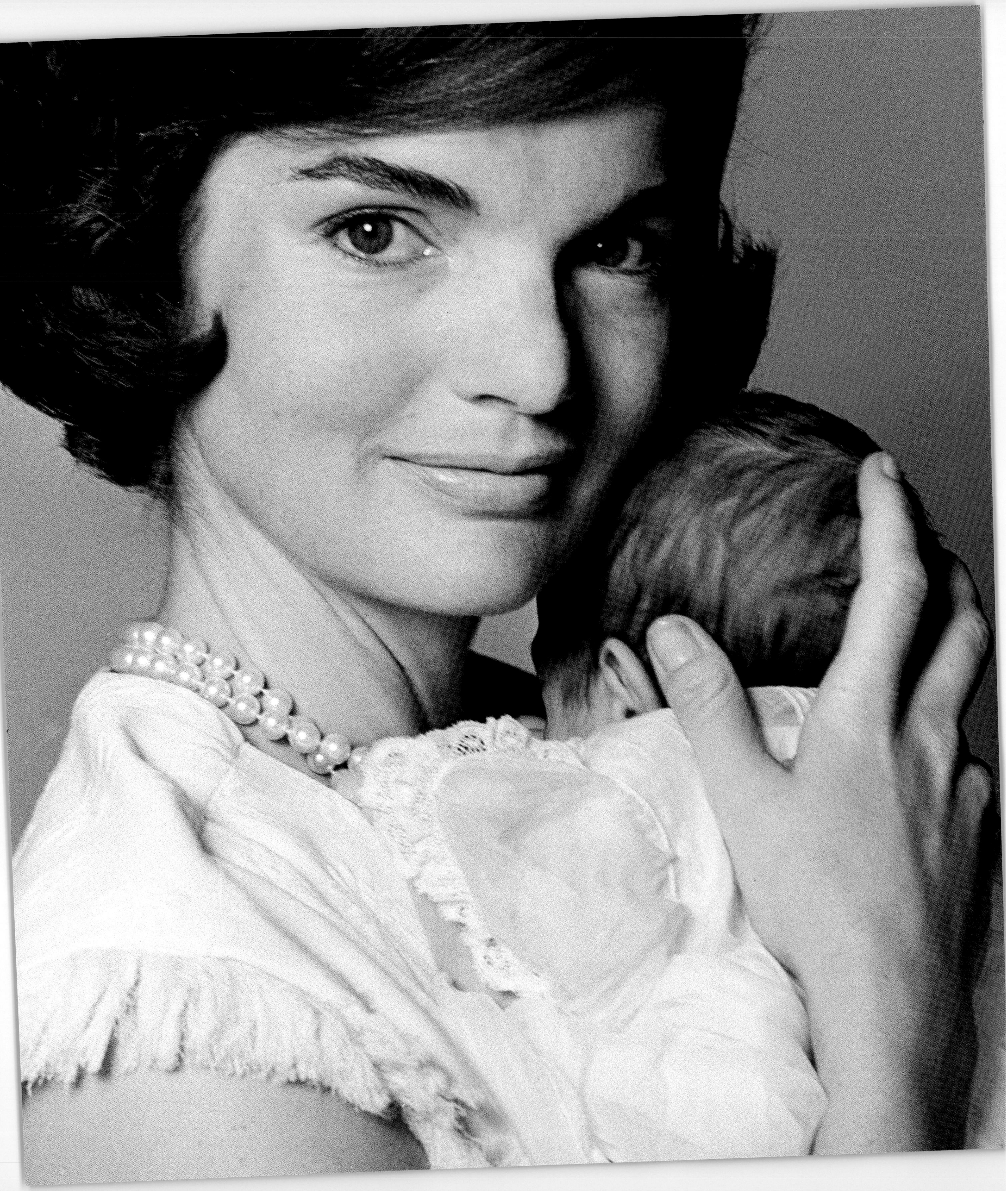

MOTHER AND SON

WATCHING A CHILD GROW, GUIDING HIM,

learning new ways to present life's

wonderful panorama of events and scenes to him—

ALL THIS IS SO WONDERFUL FOR THE PARENT.

—Jacqueline Kennedy, "Your Child's World," *Times-Herald*, December 11, 1960

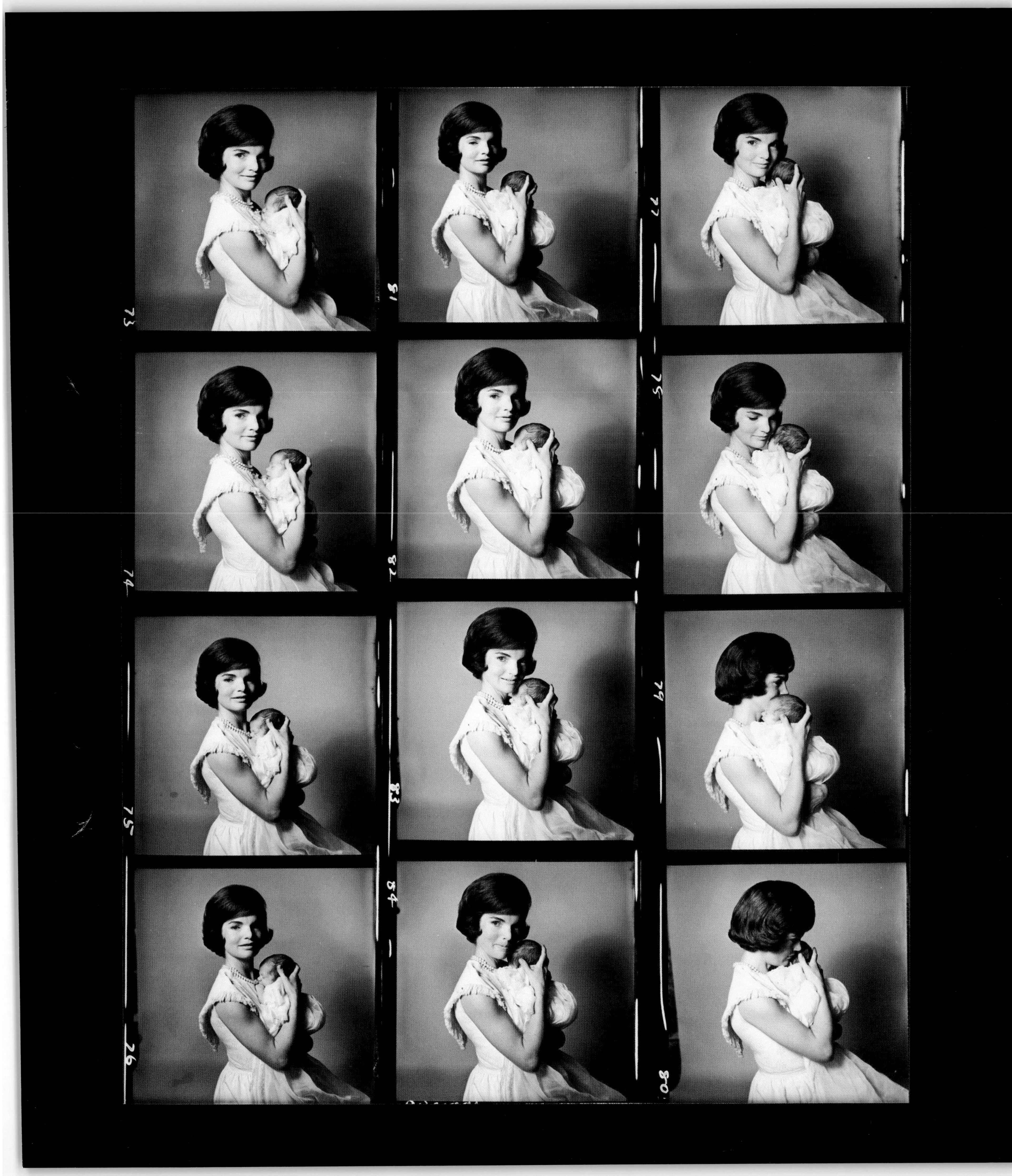

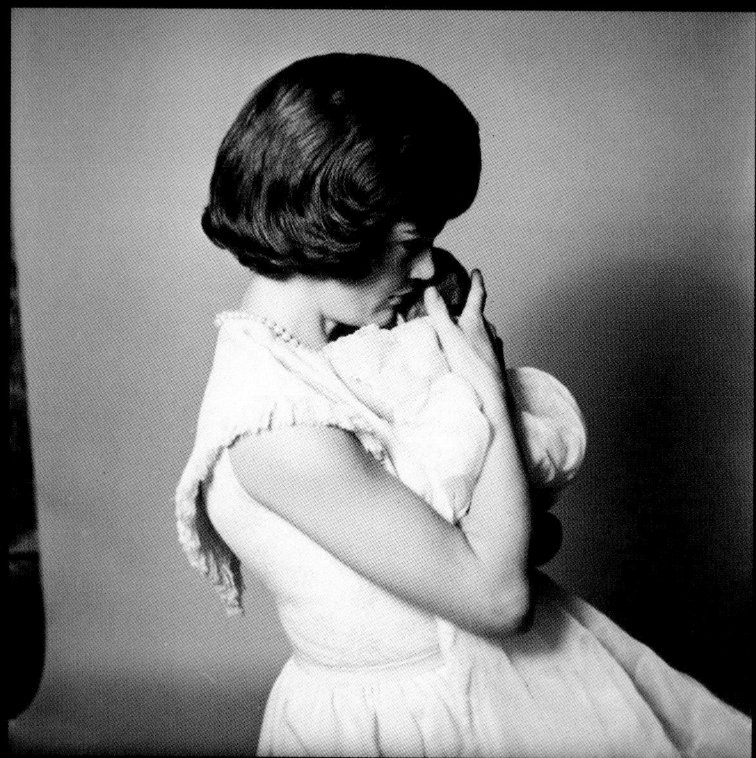

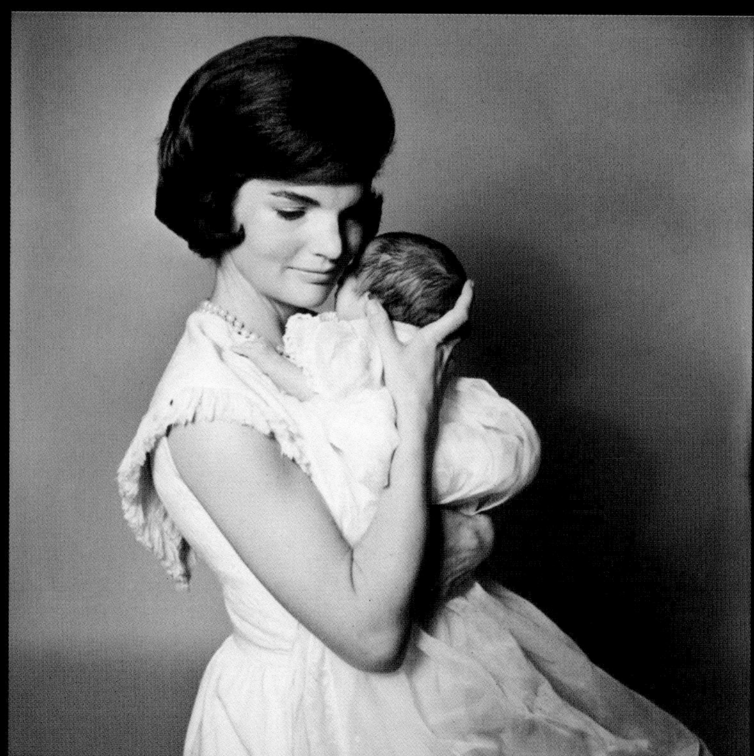

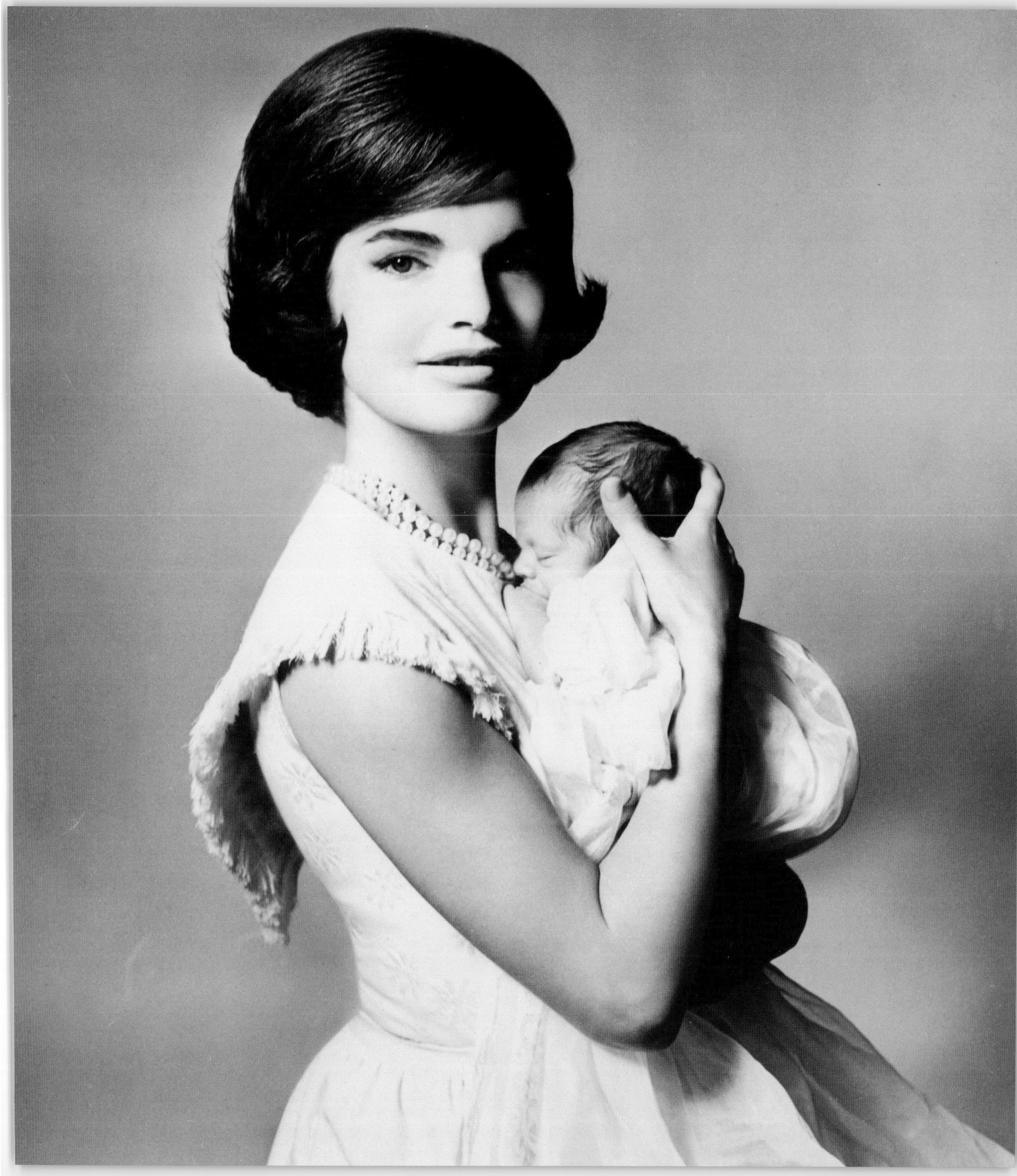

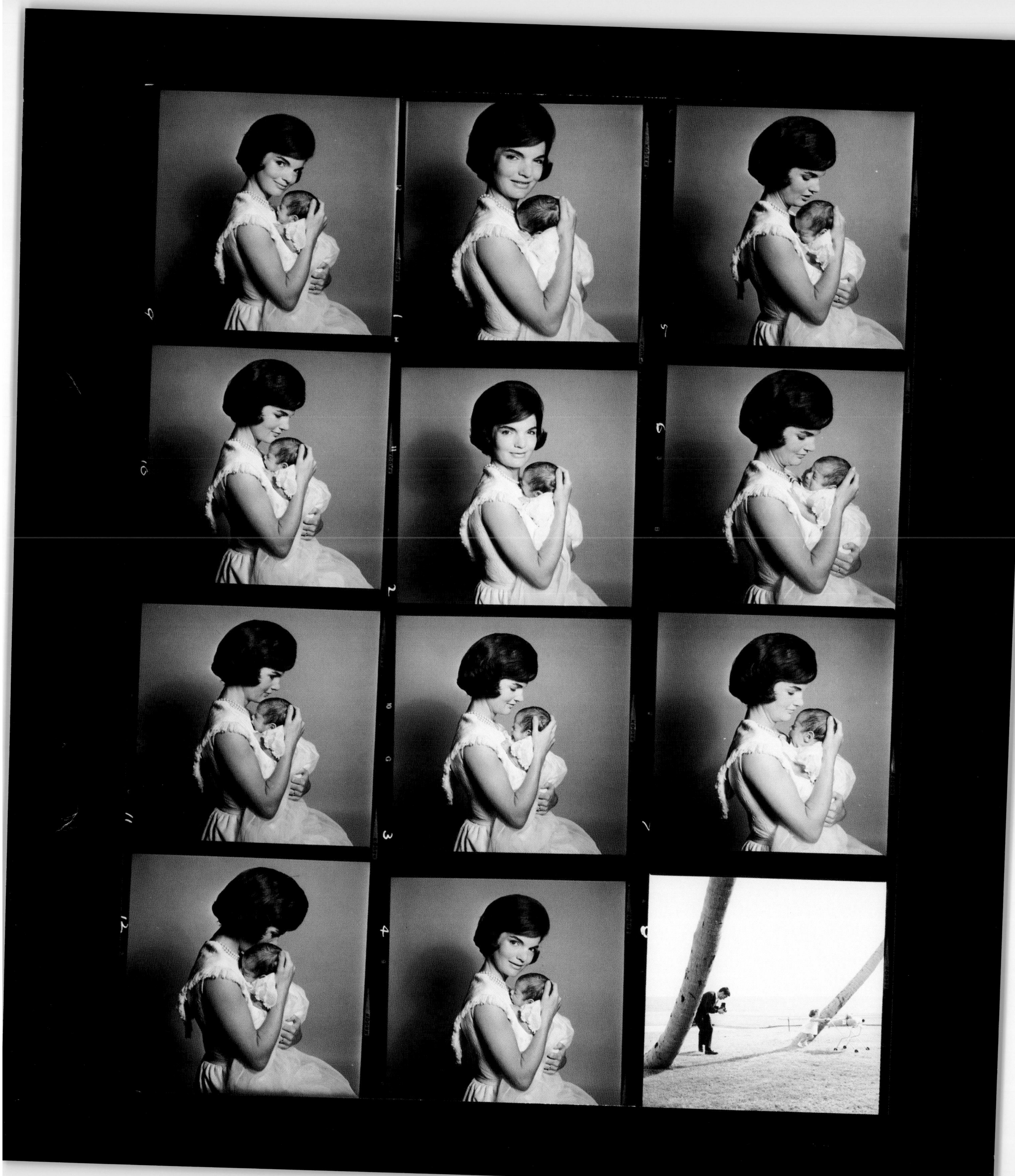

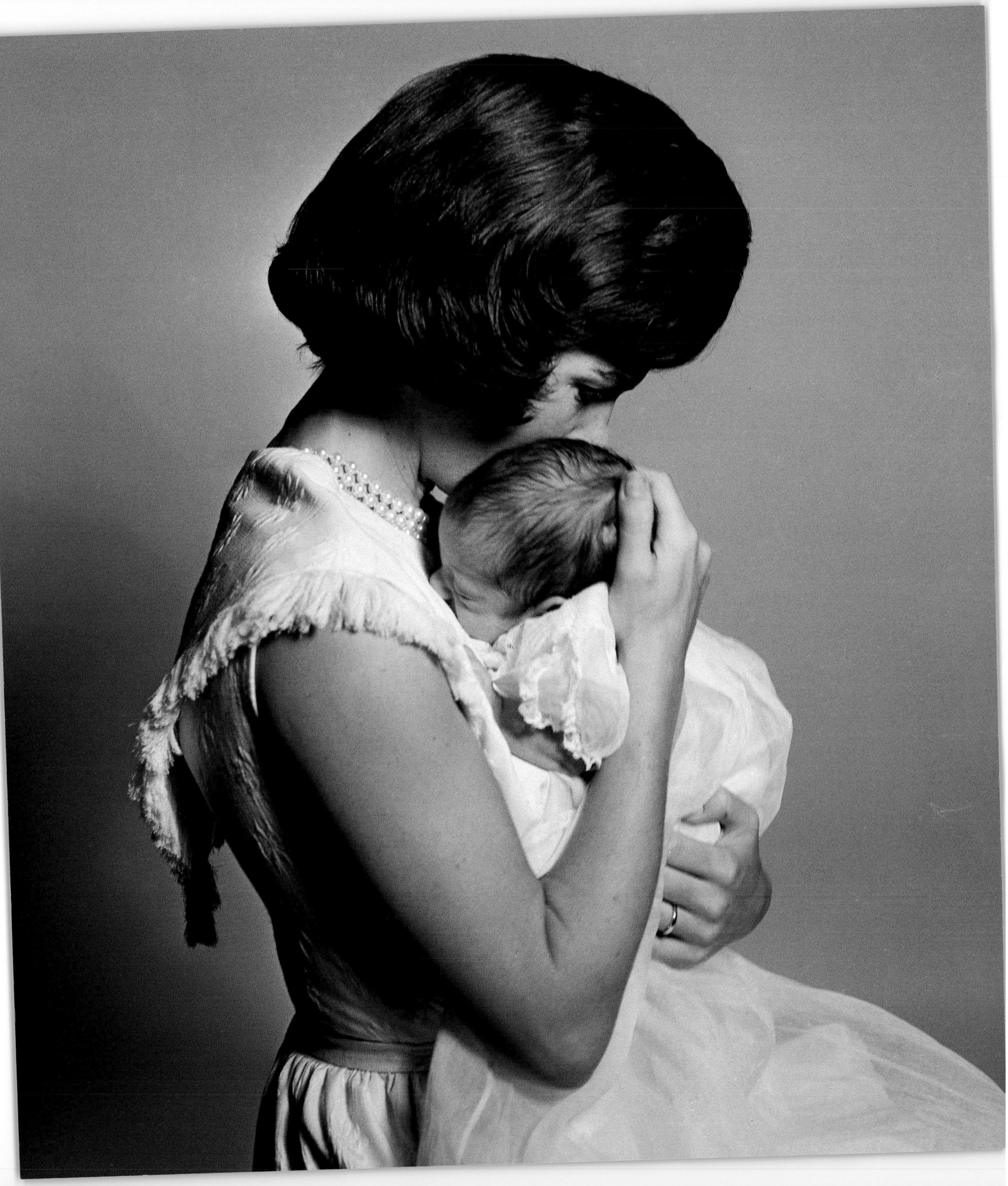

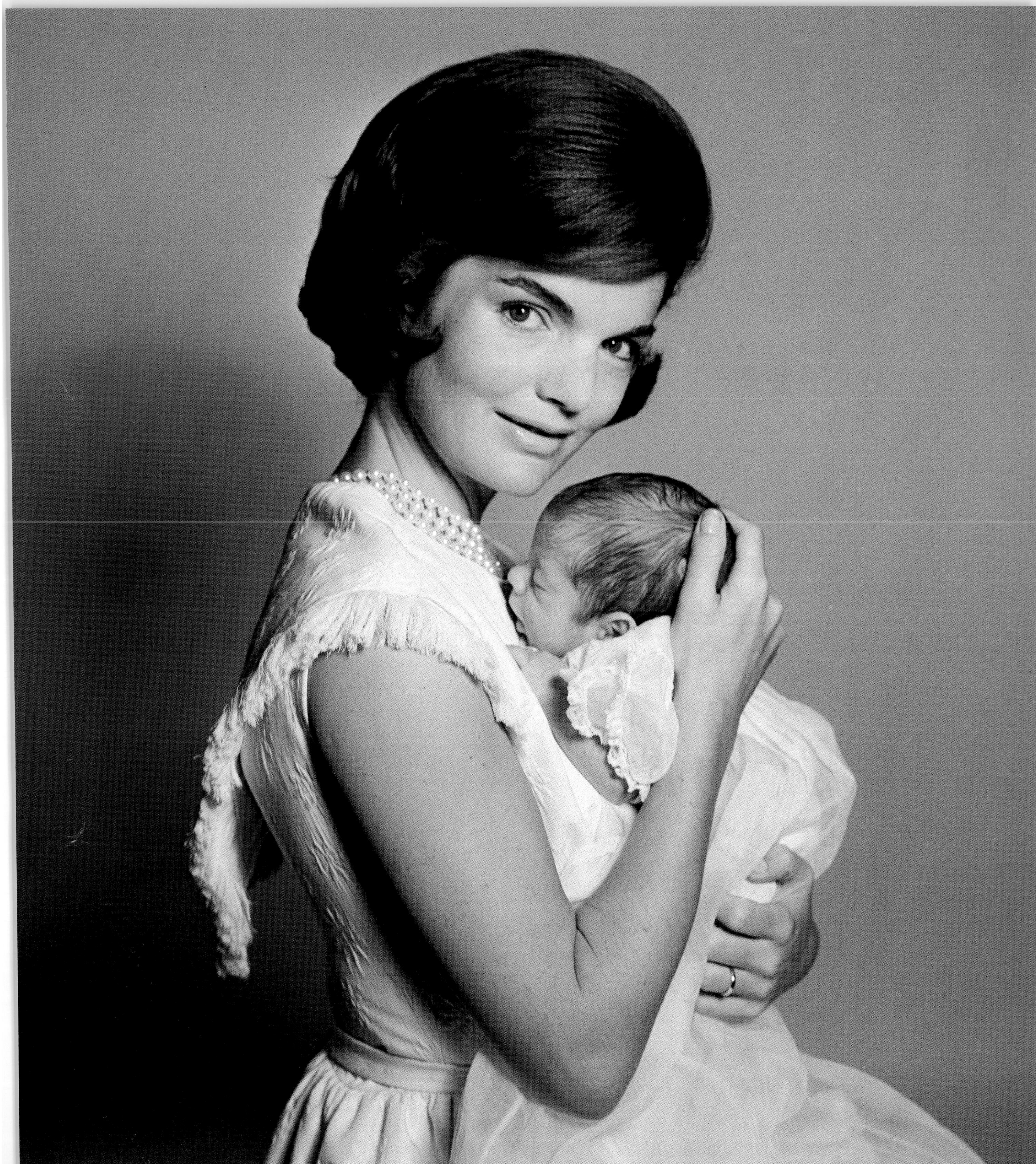

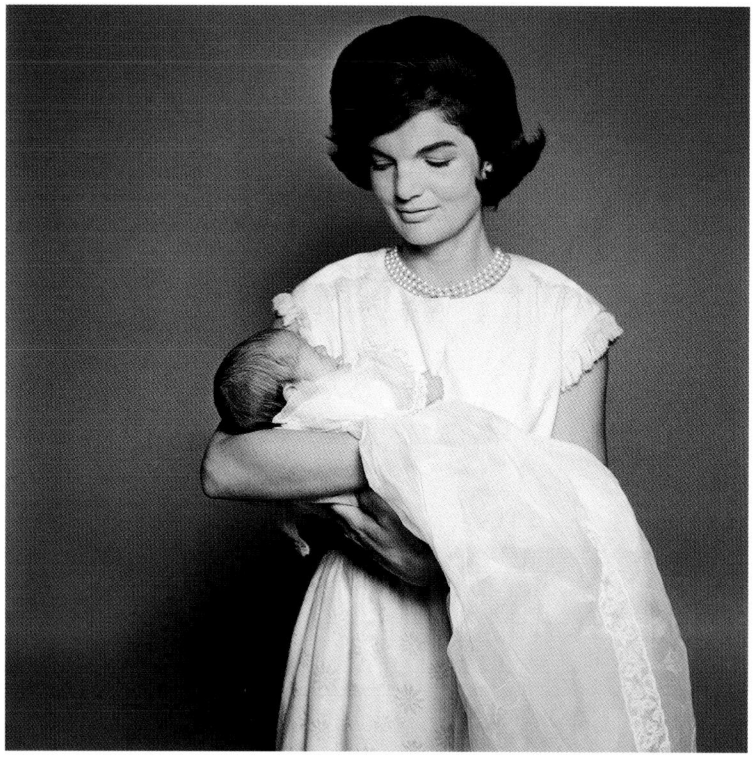

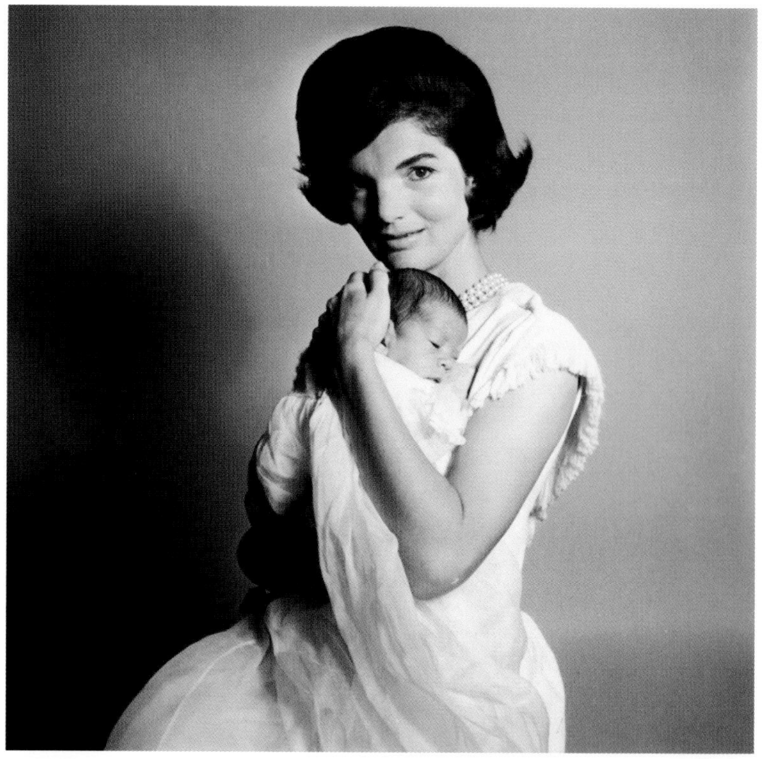

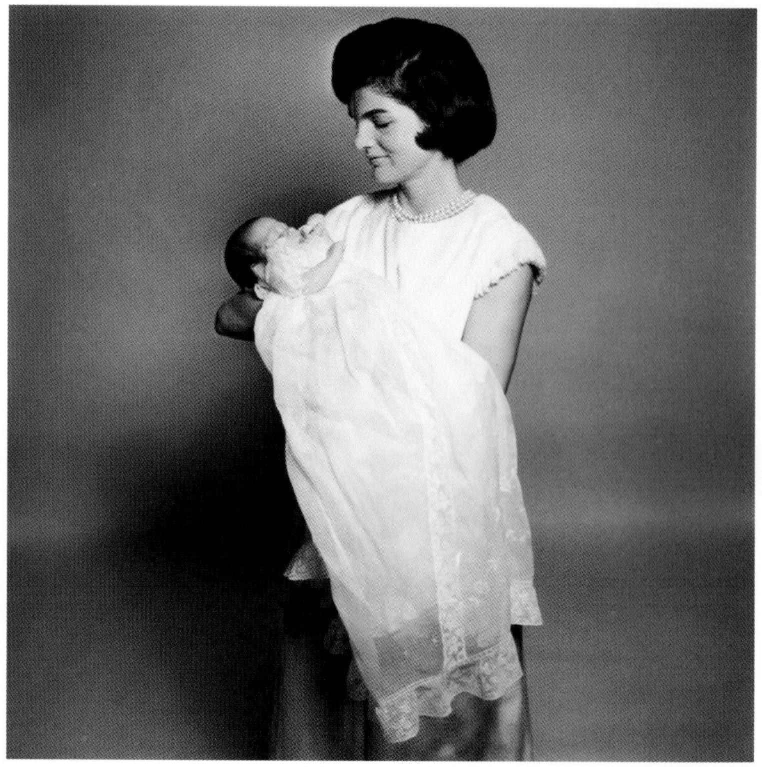

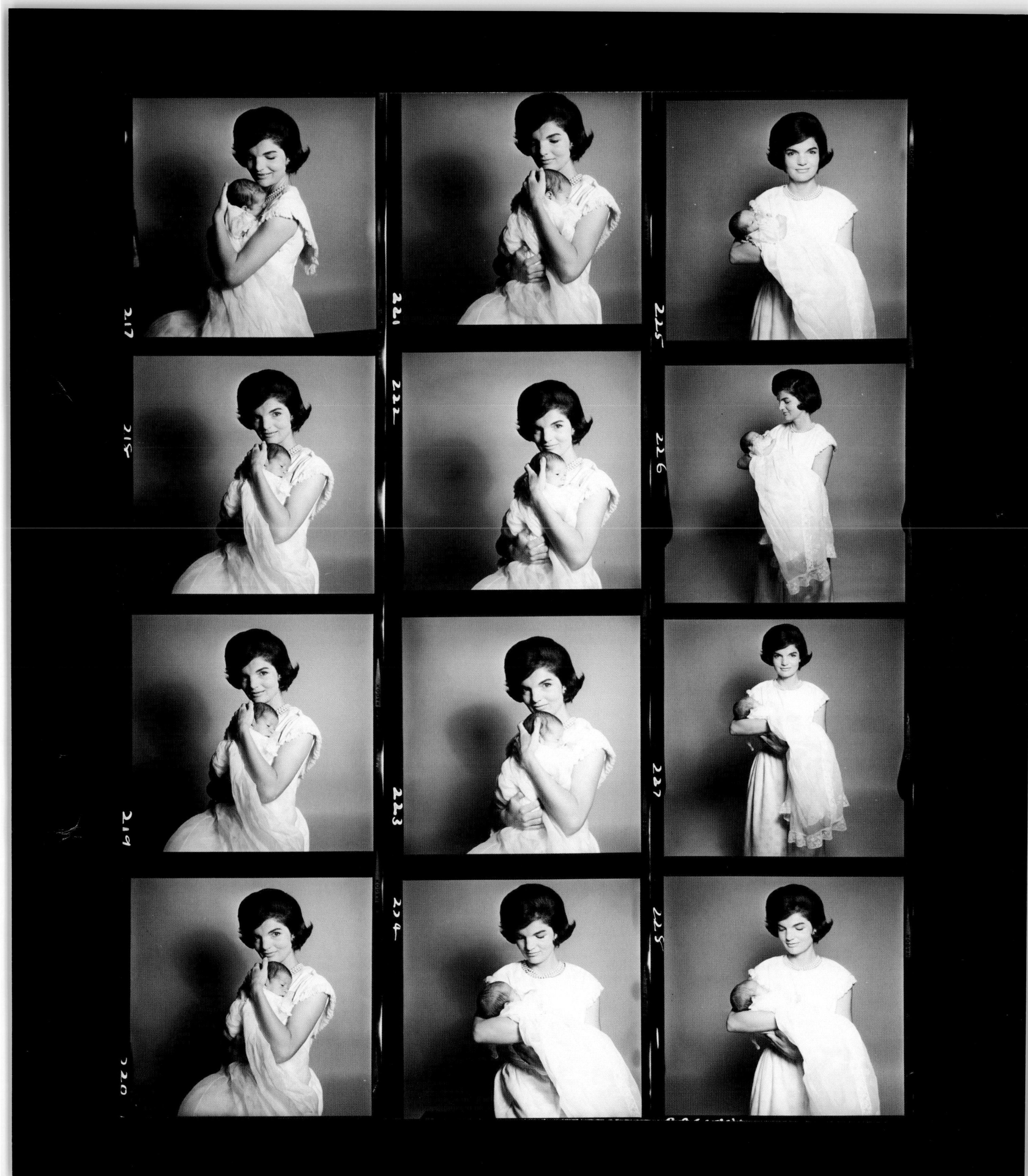

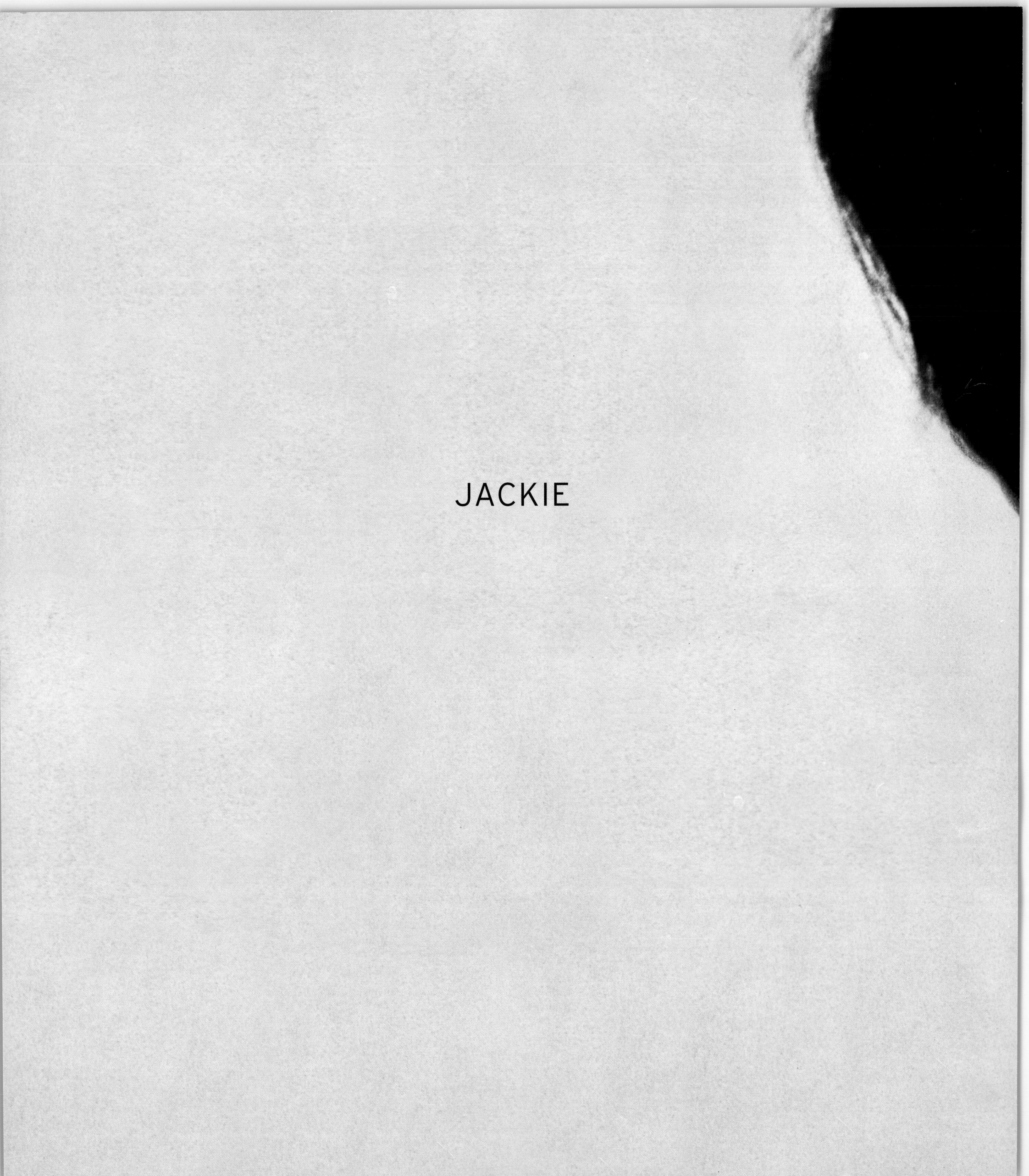

JACKIE

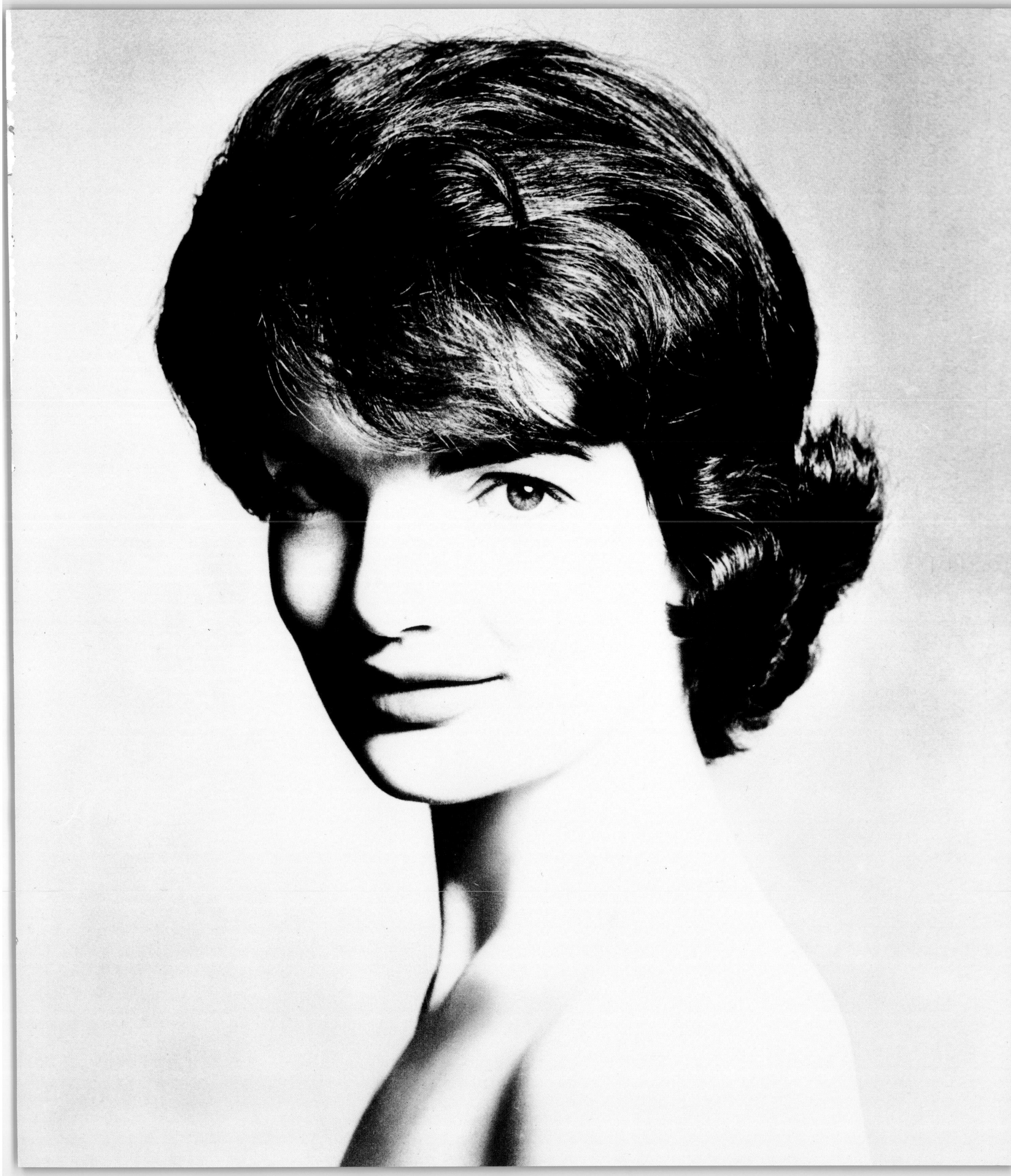

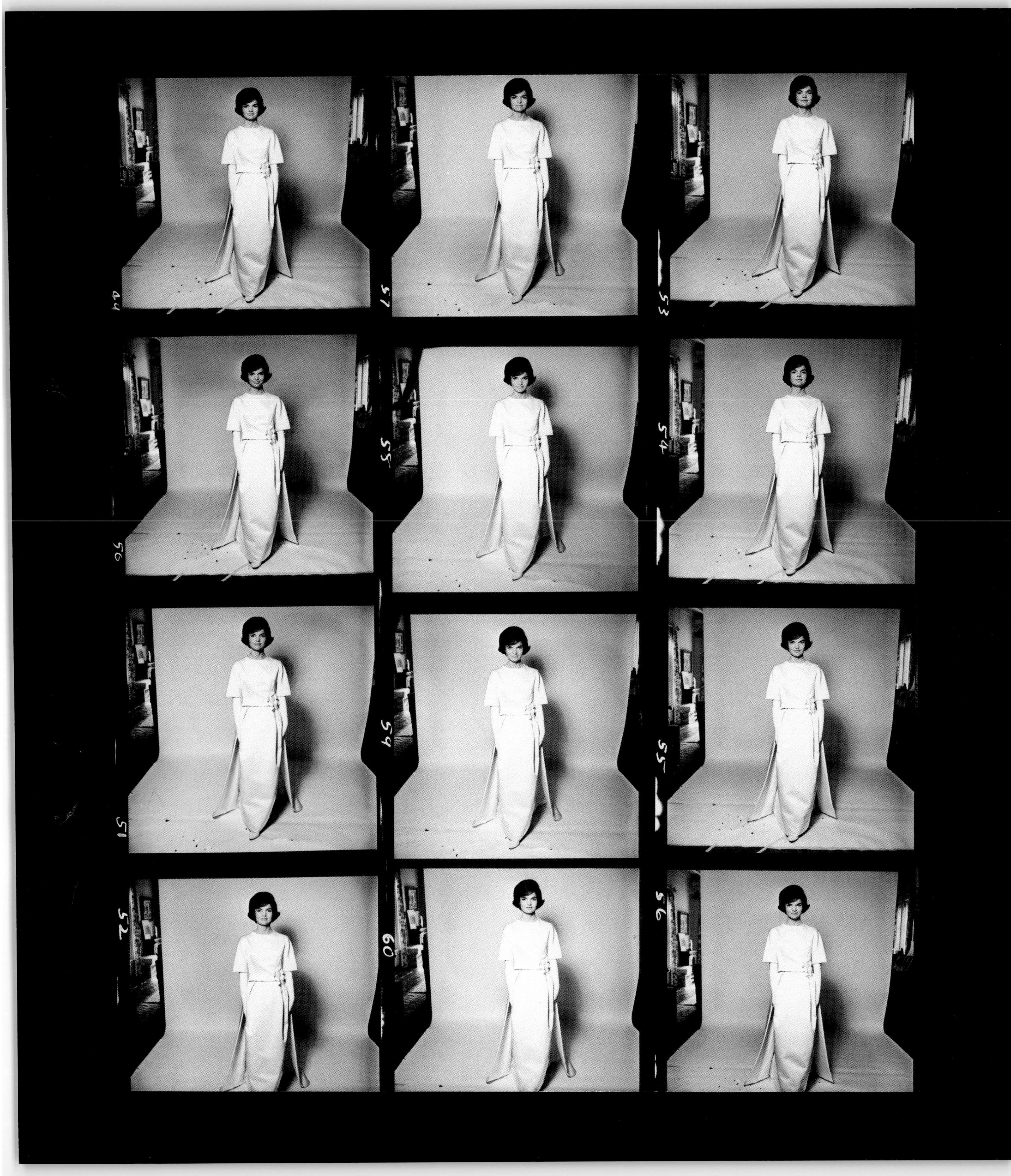

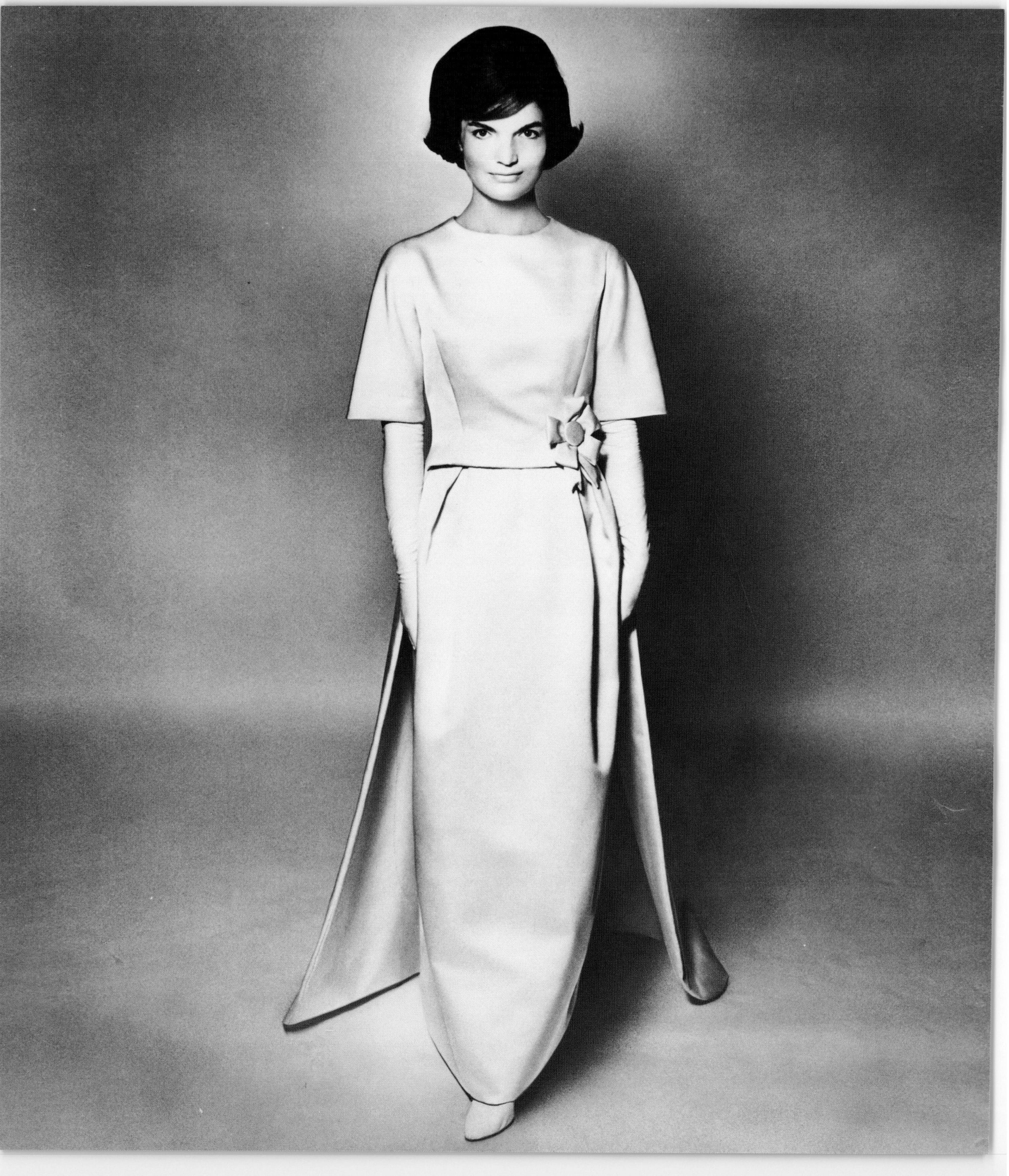

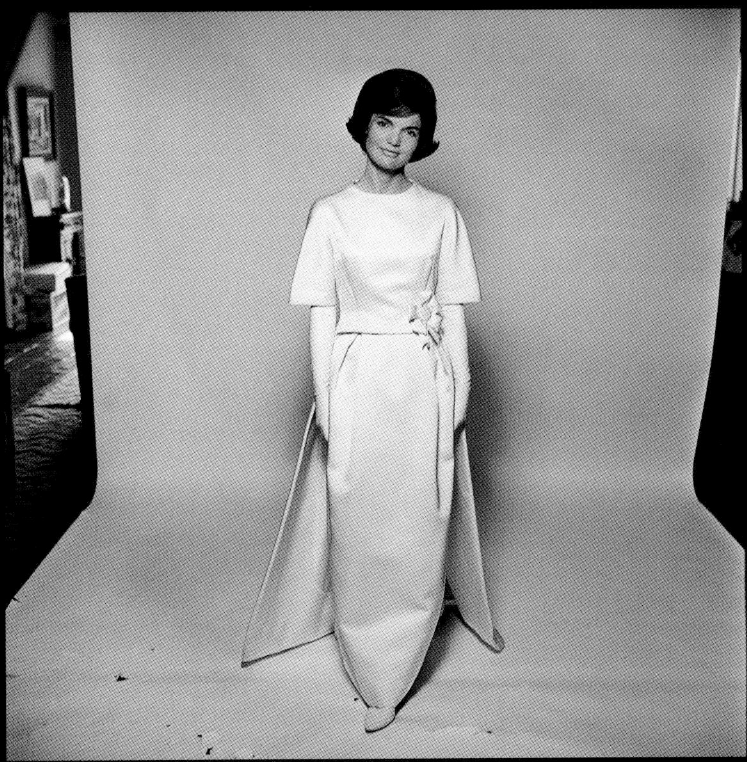

JACQUELINE IS RAVISHING.

Today she's THE MOST BEAUTIFUL WOMAN IN THE WORLD.

She has a great deal in common with the top movie stars—

SHE KNOWS WHEN TO HOLD HERSELF BACK

while everyone else you know gives too much of themselves at one time.

So when she comes out, it's A GREAT TOUR DE FORCE.

—Richard Avedon in "Look at the Birdie," *Newsweek*, February 6, 1961

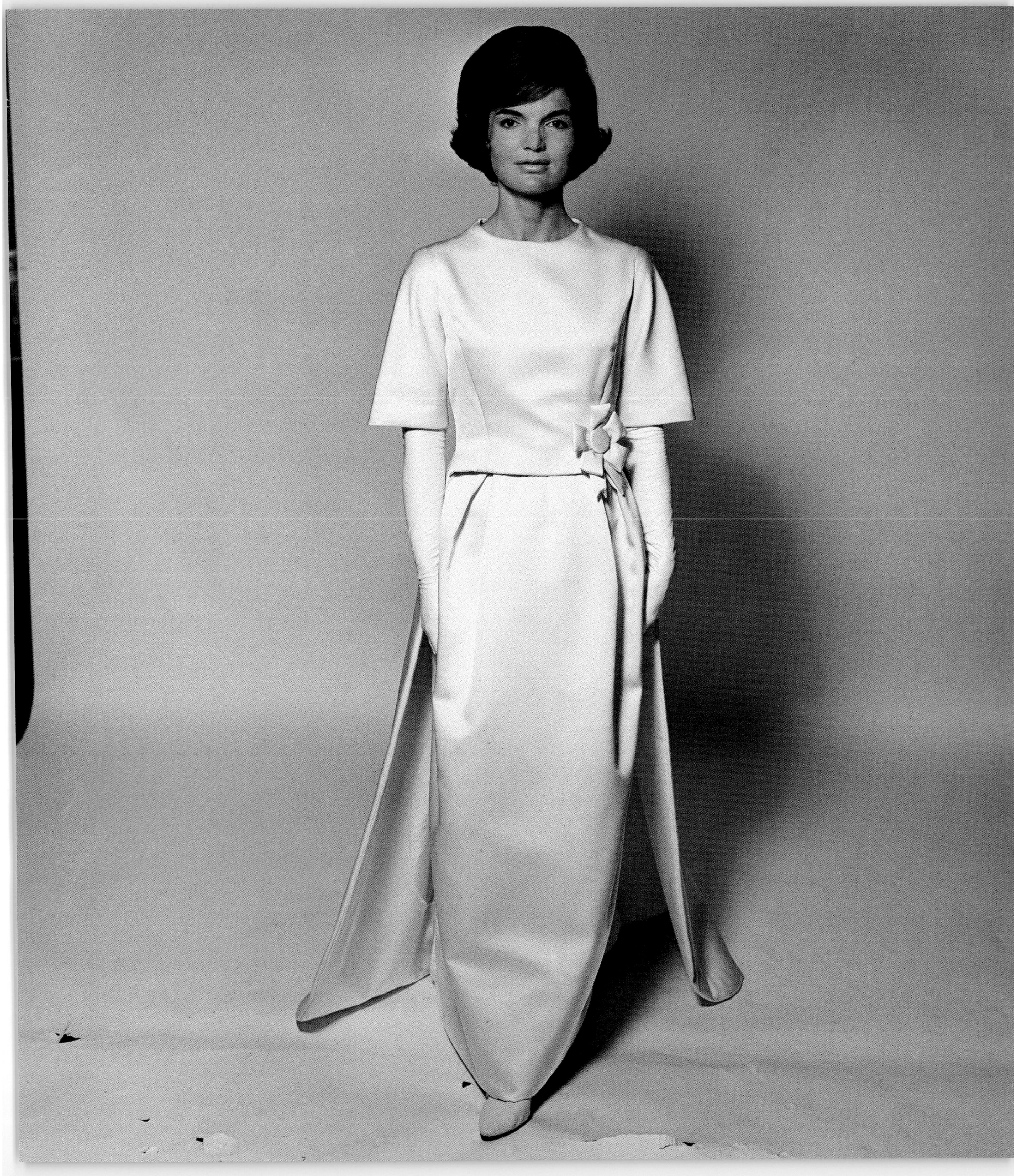

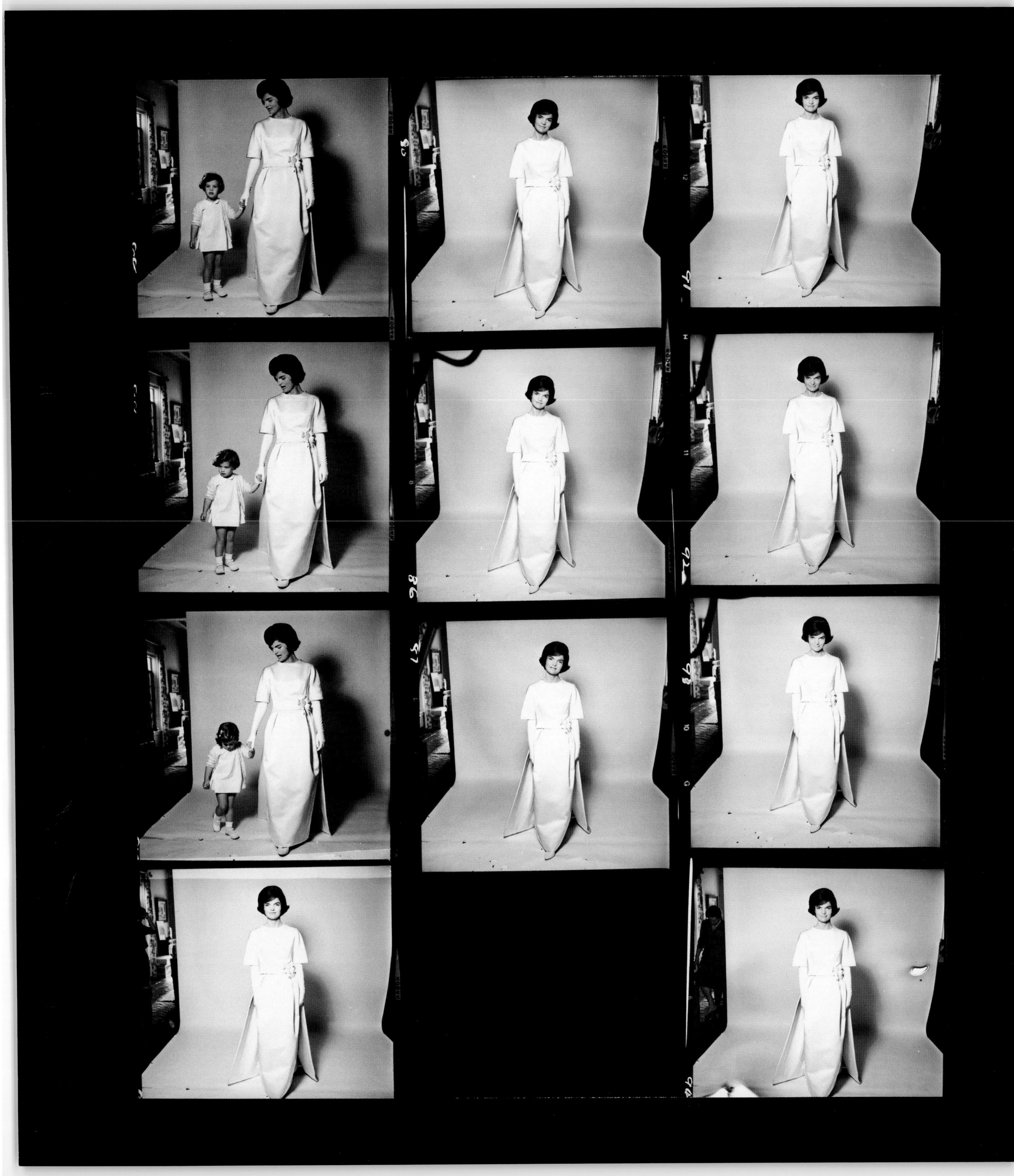

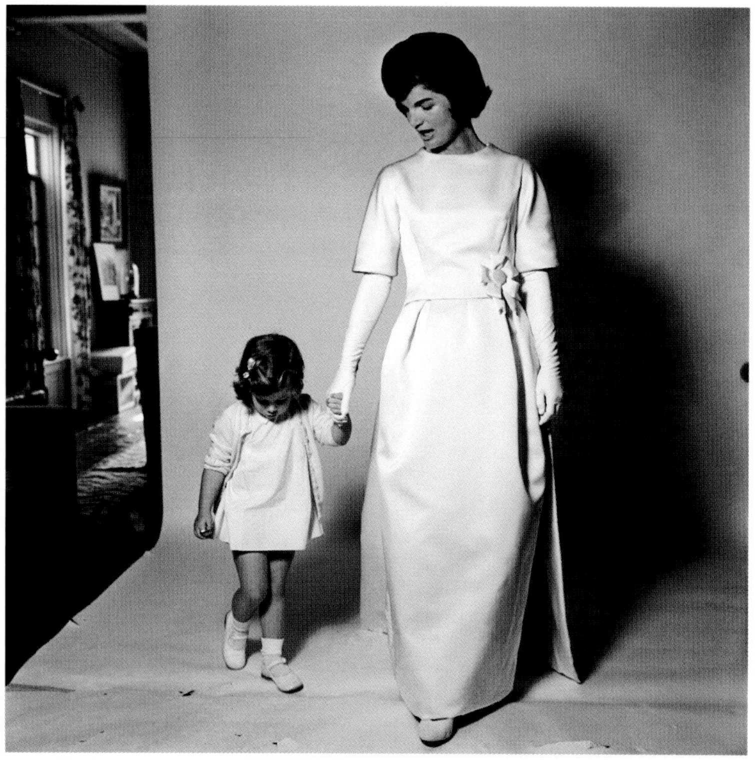

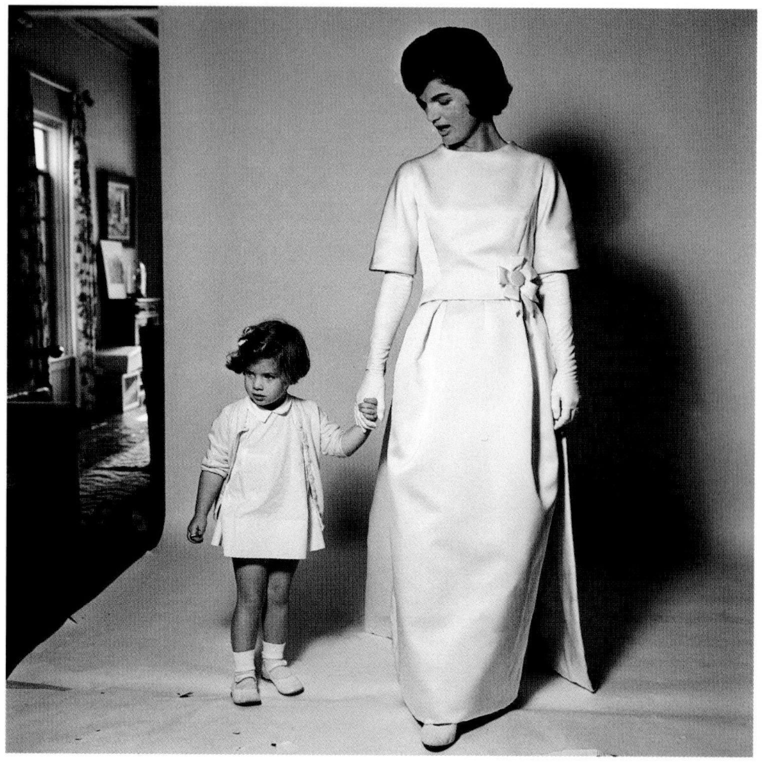

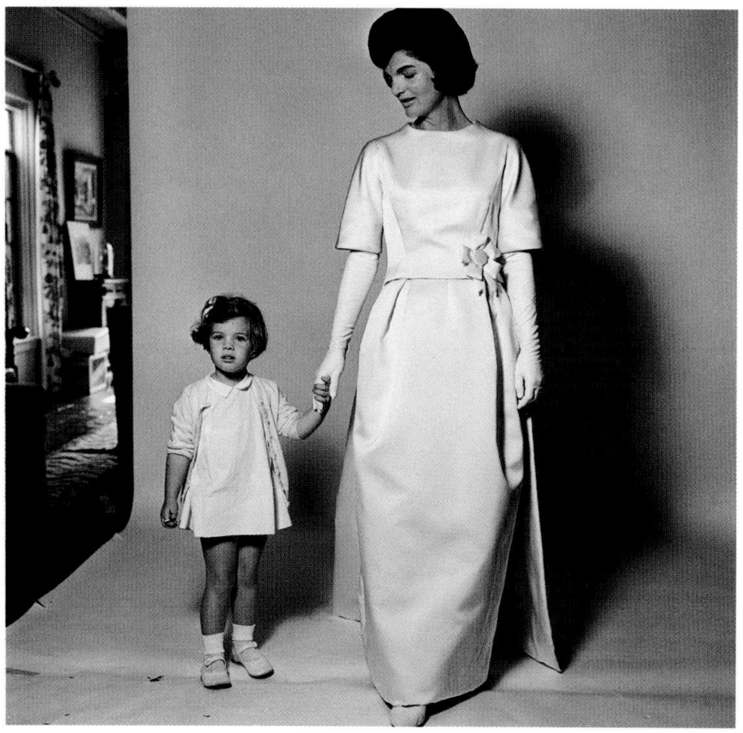

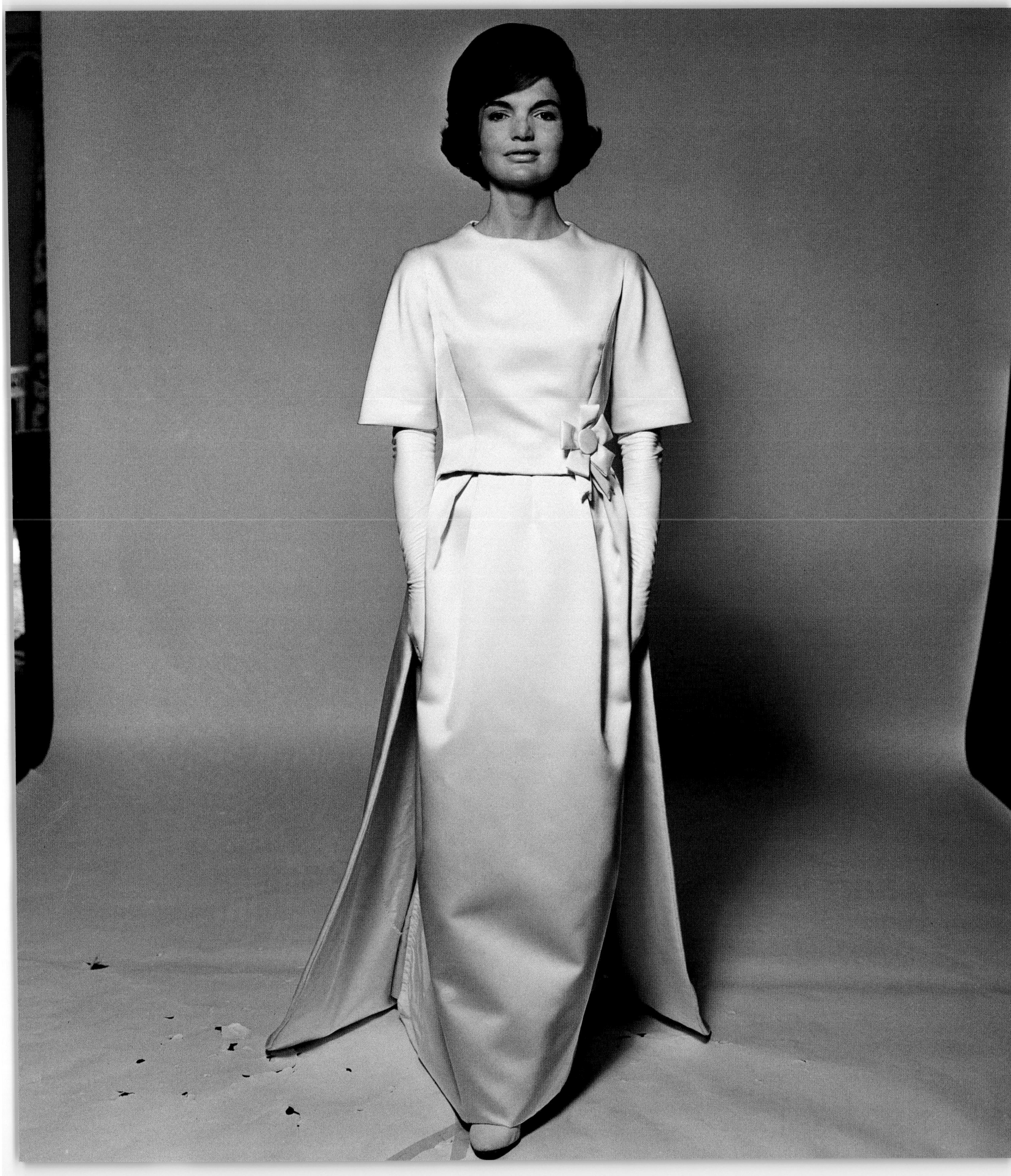

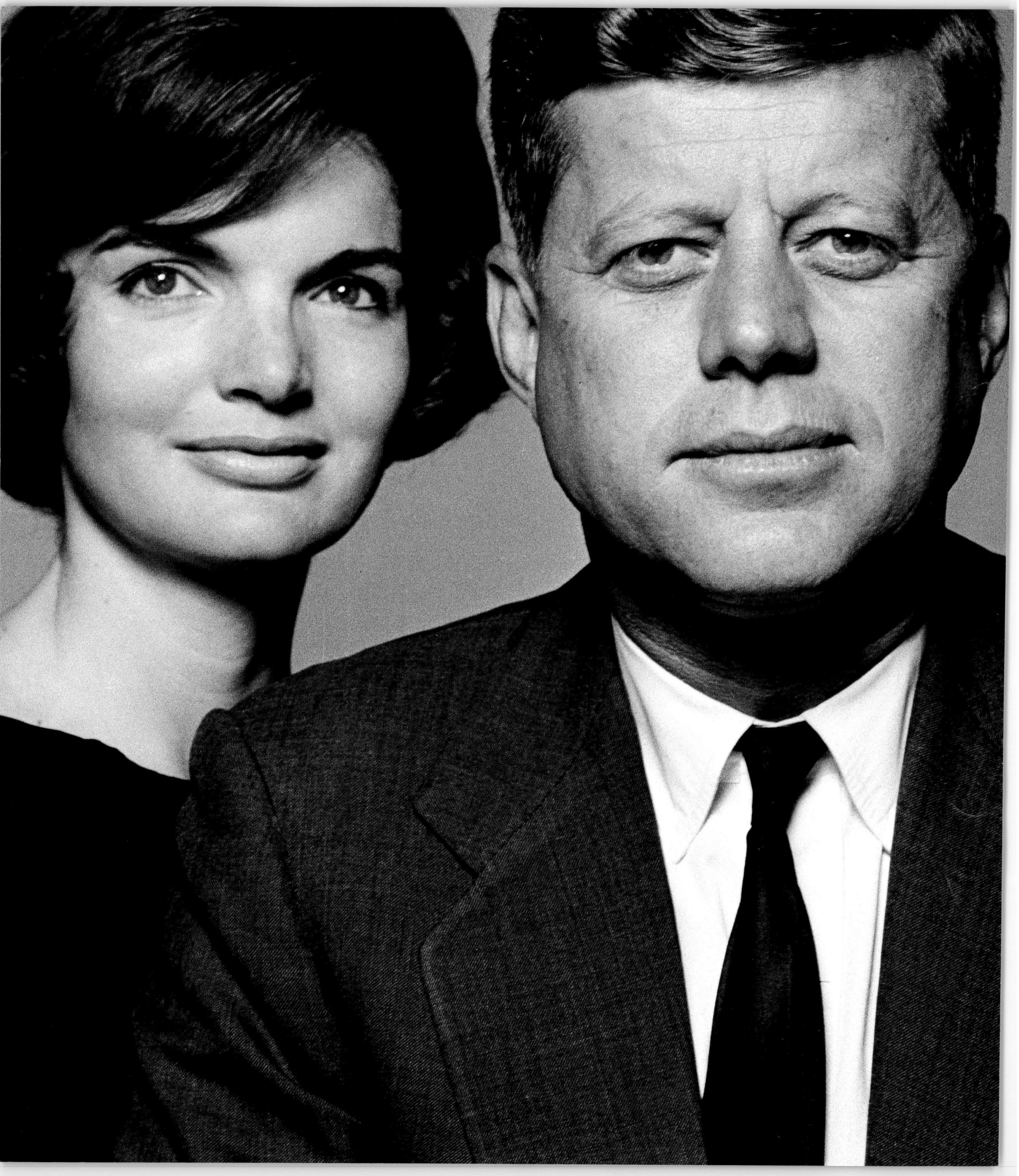

HUSBAND AND WIFE

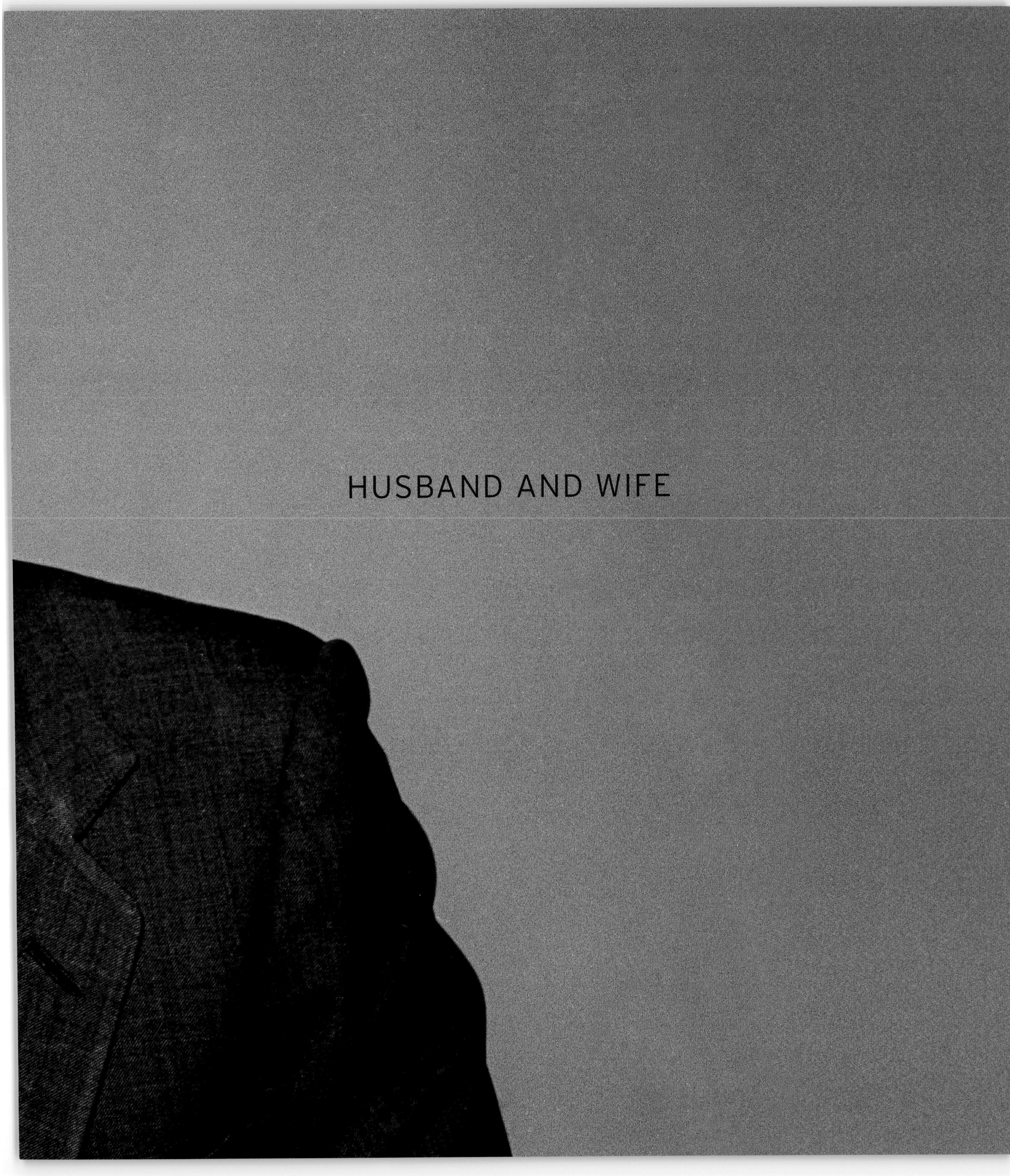

In a very charming way, he was ill at ease....

JACQUELINE SAID HE ALWAYS LOOKS HIS BEST

WHEN HE'S TALKING TO A CROWD,

and freezes up when he has his portrait taken.

—Richard Avedon in "Look at the Birdie," *Newsweek*, February 6, 1961

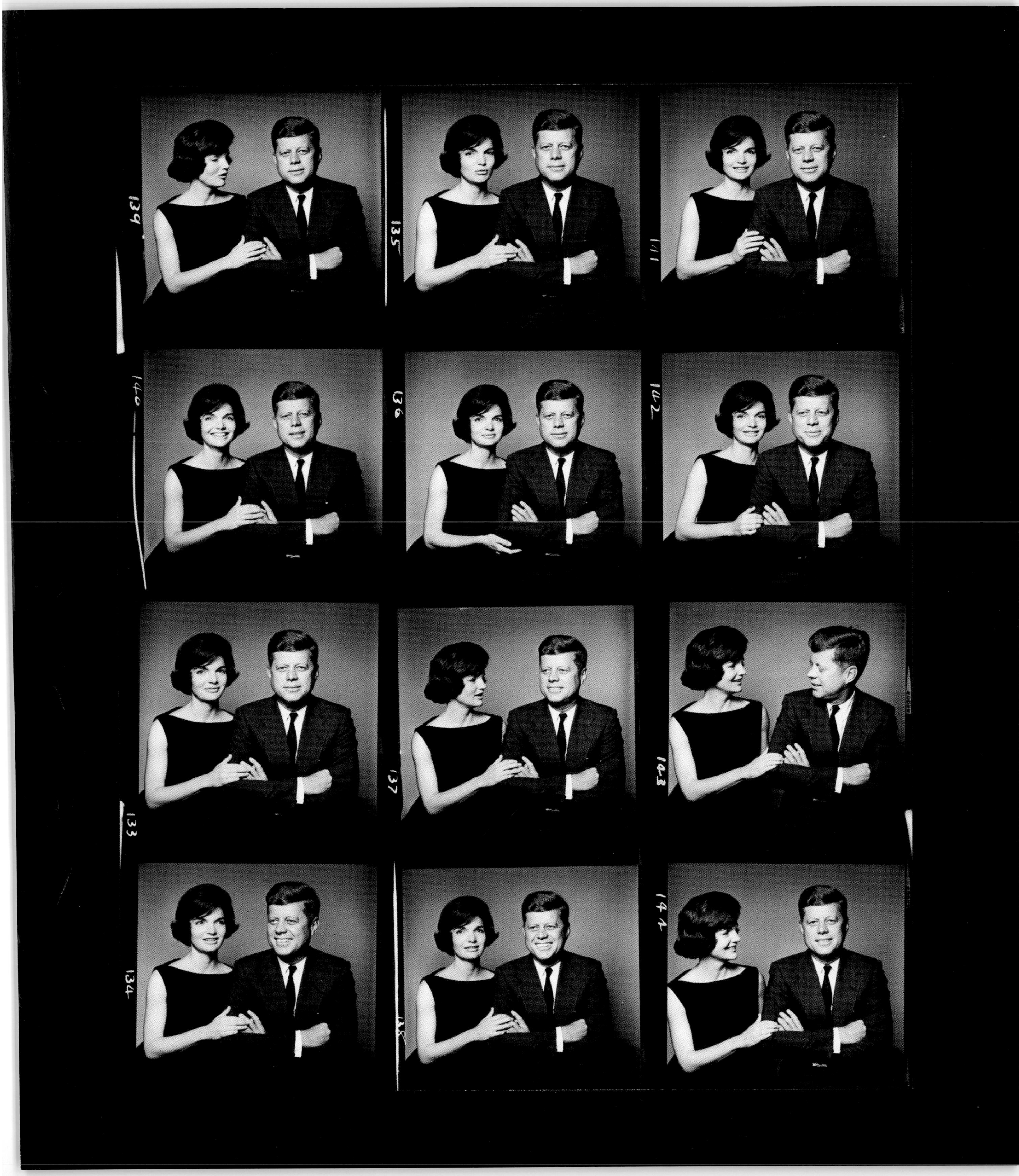

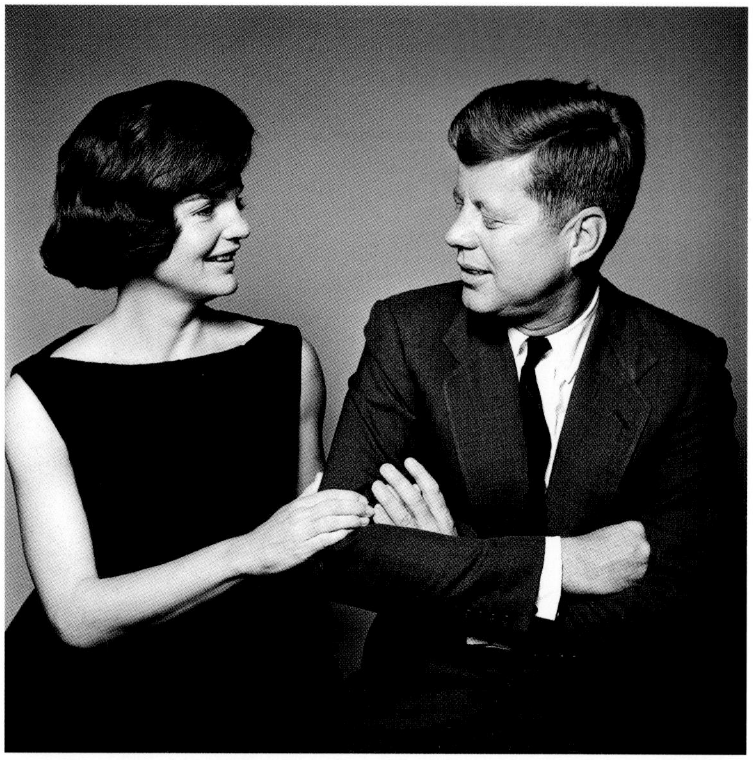

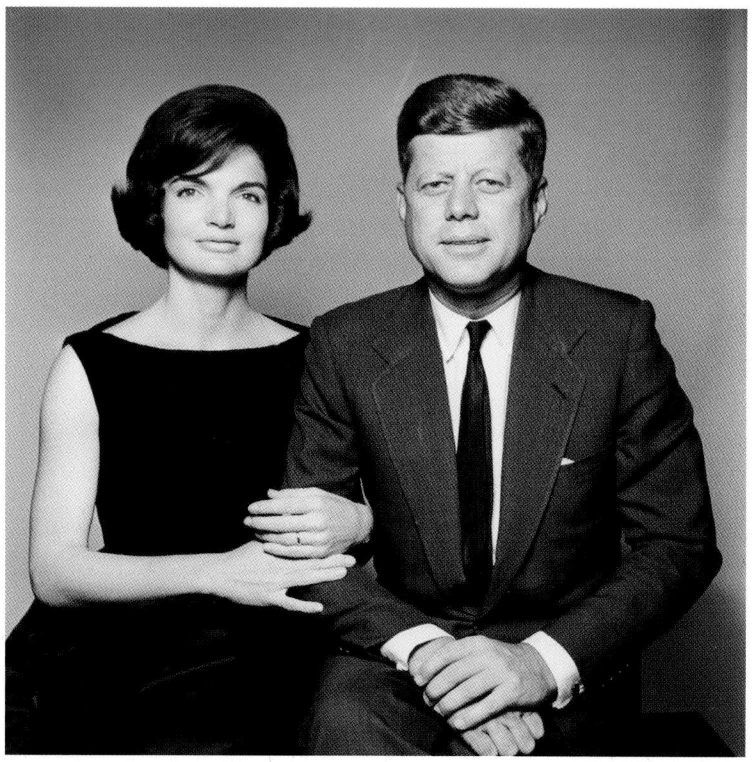

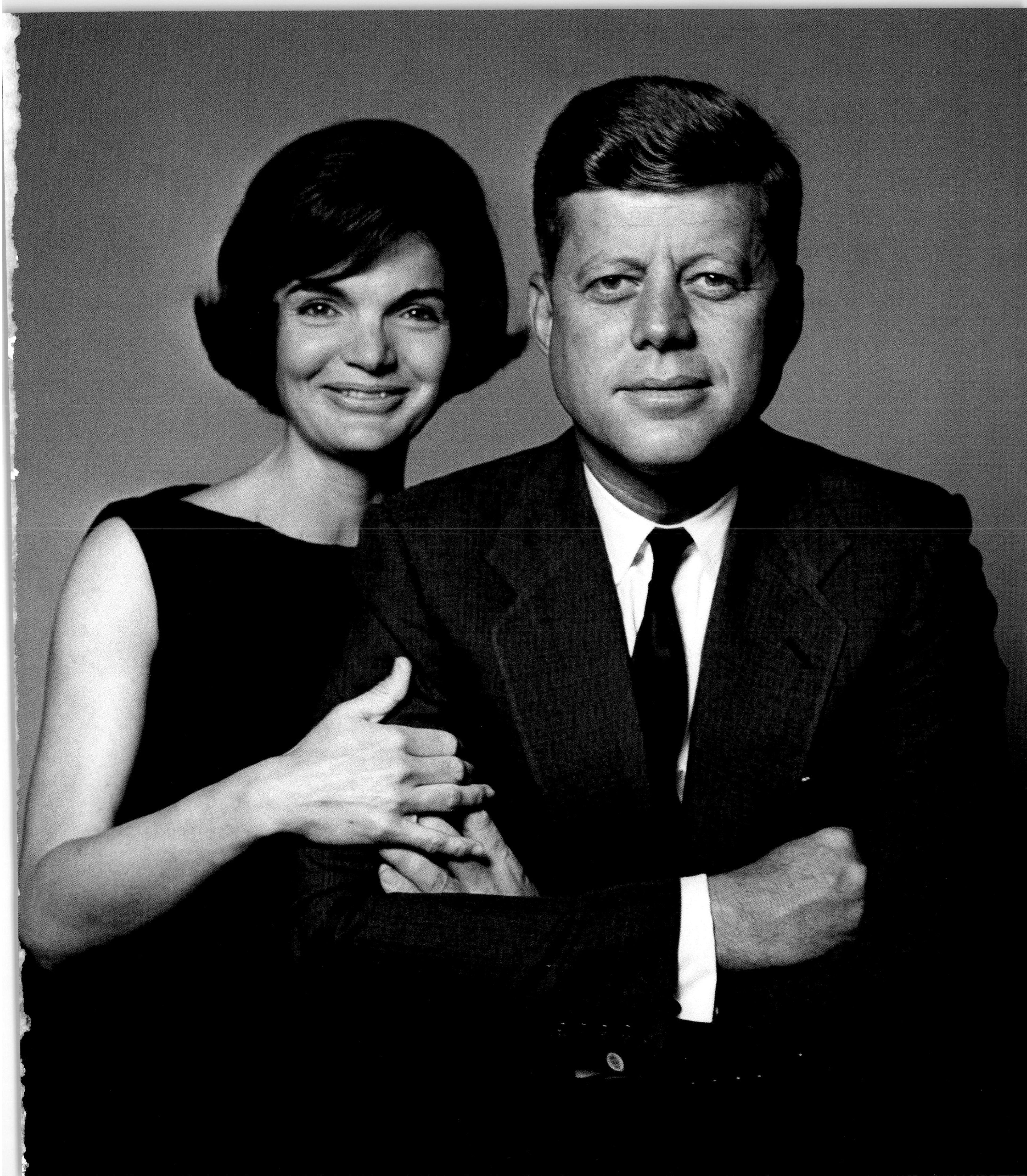

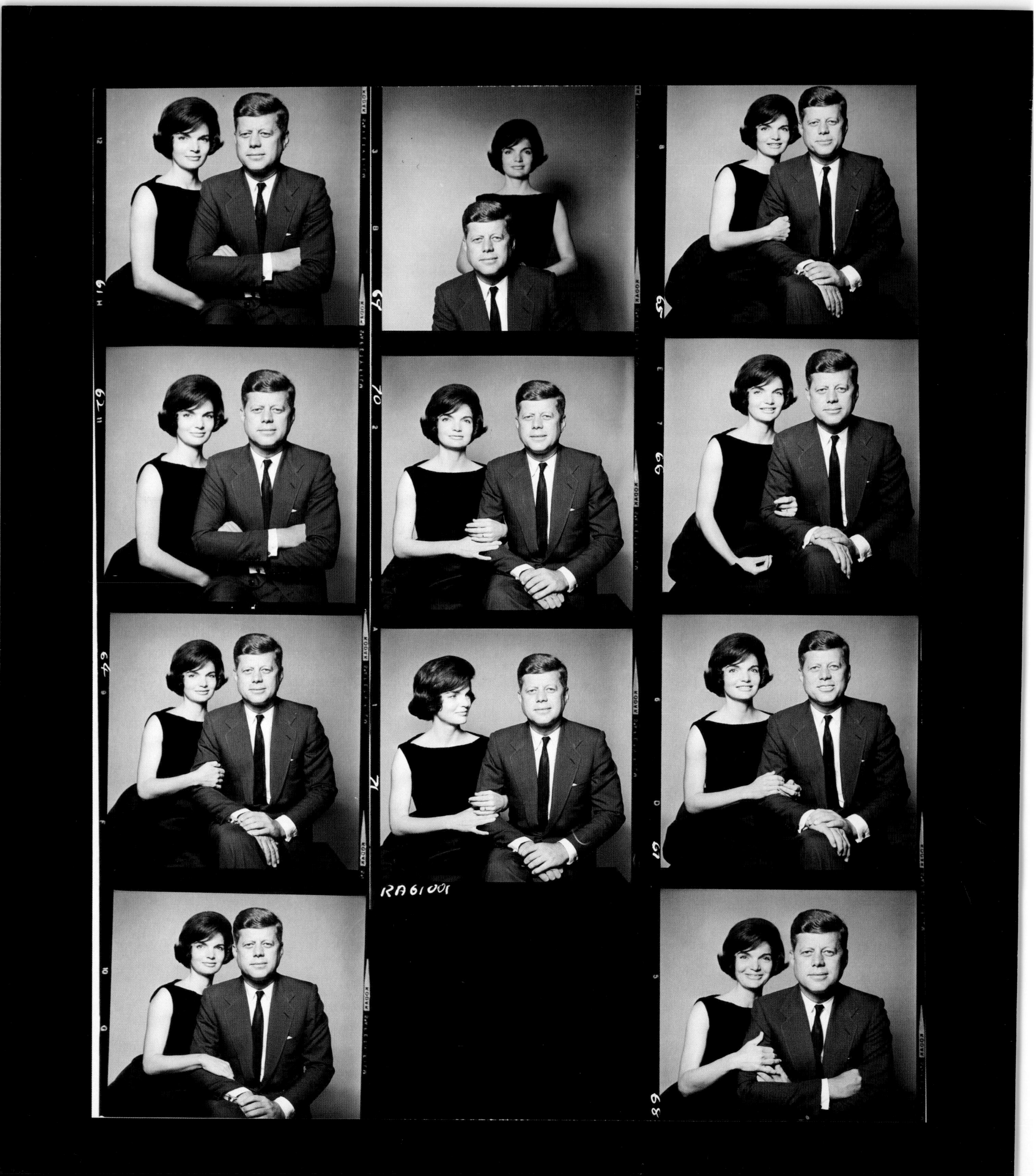
RA61001

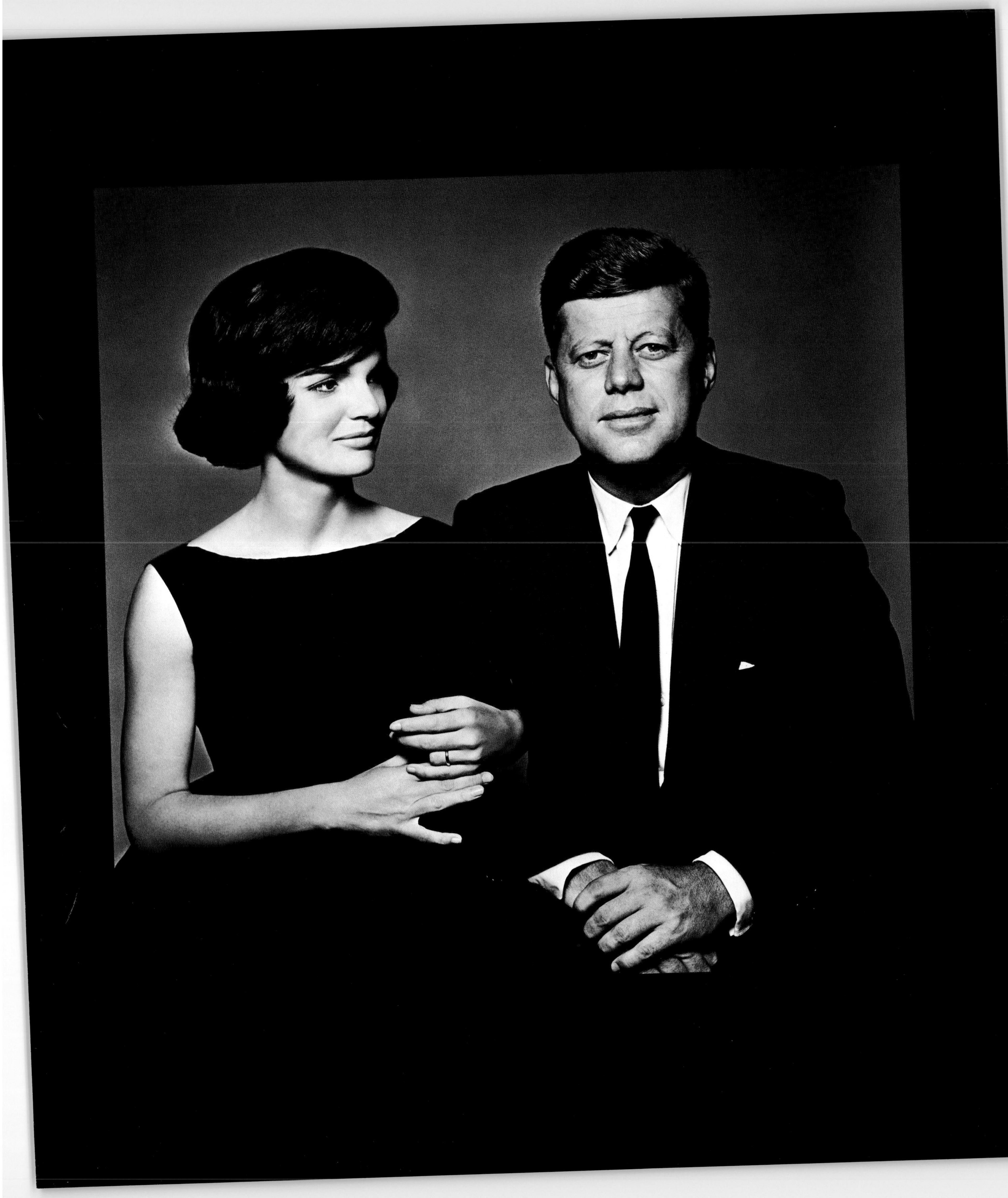

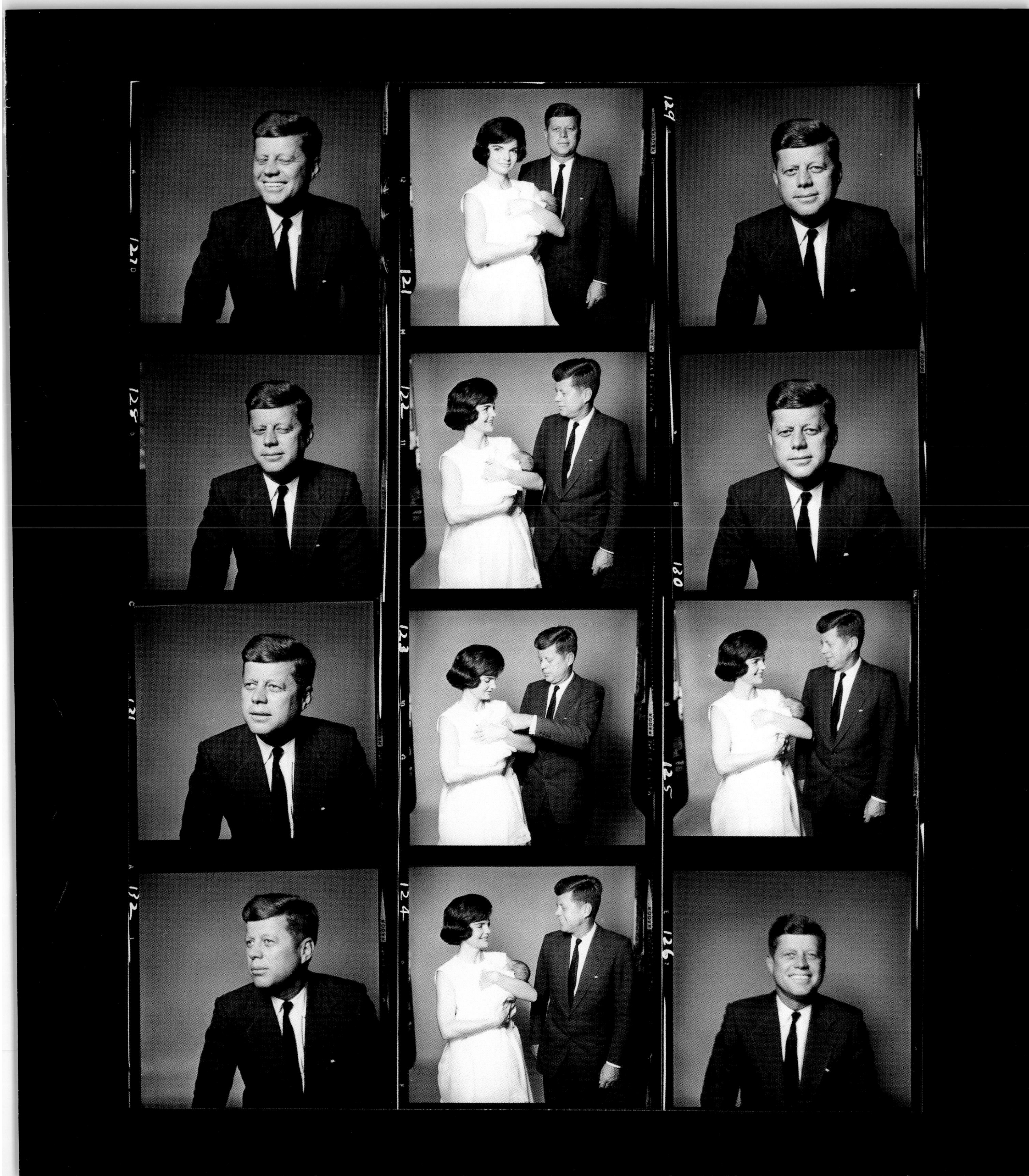

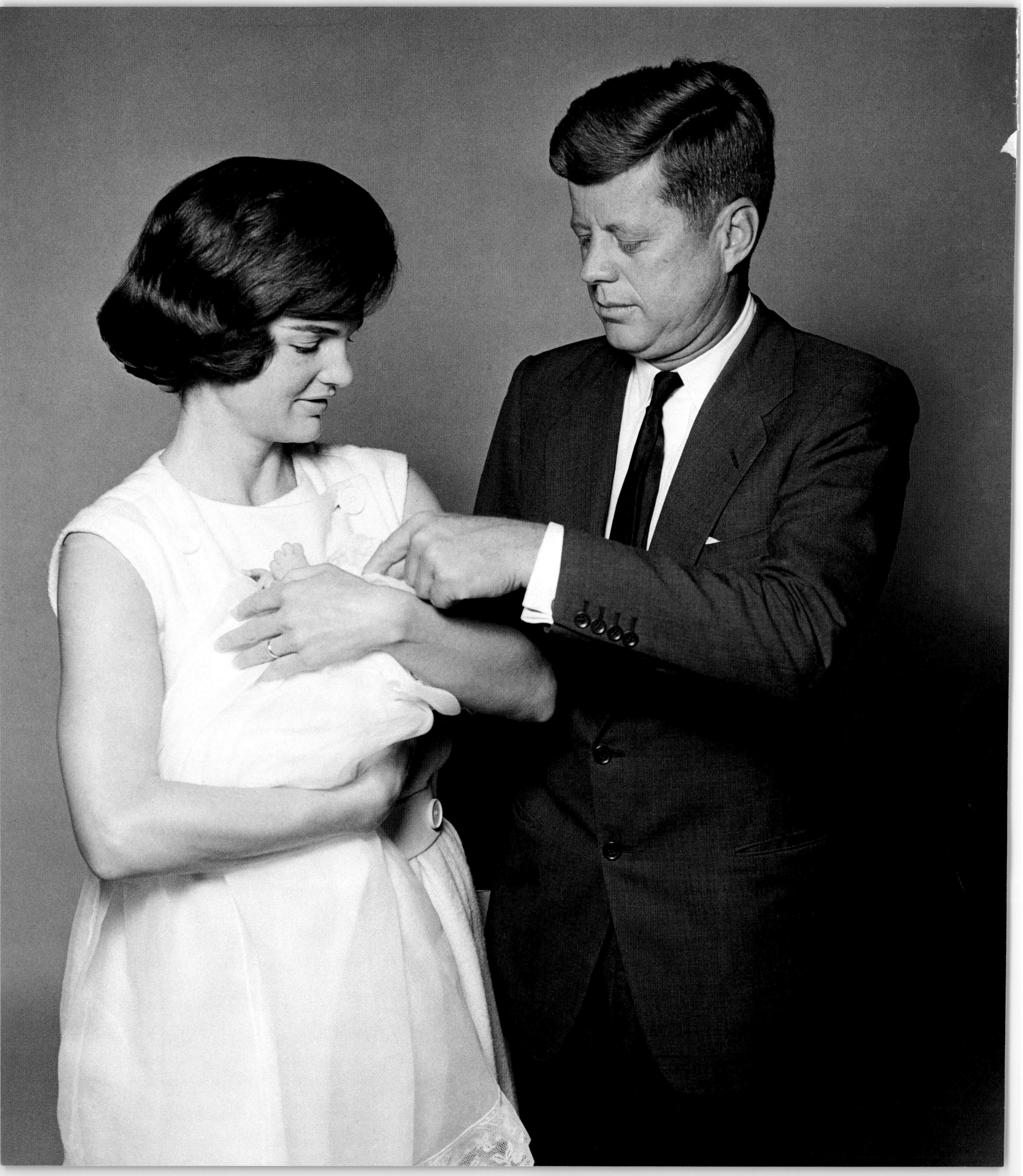

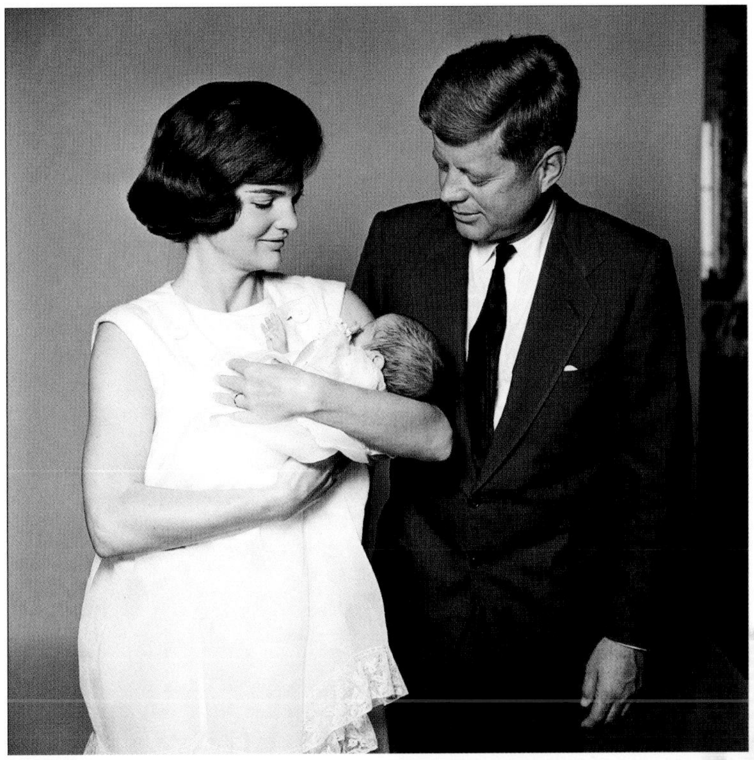

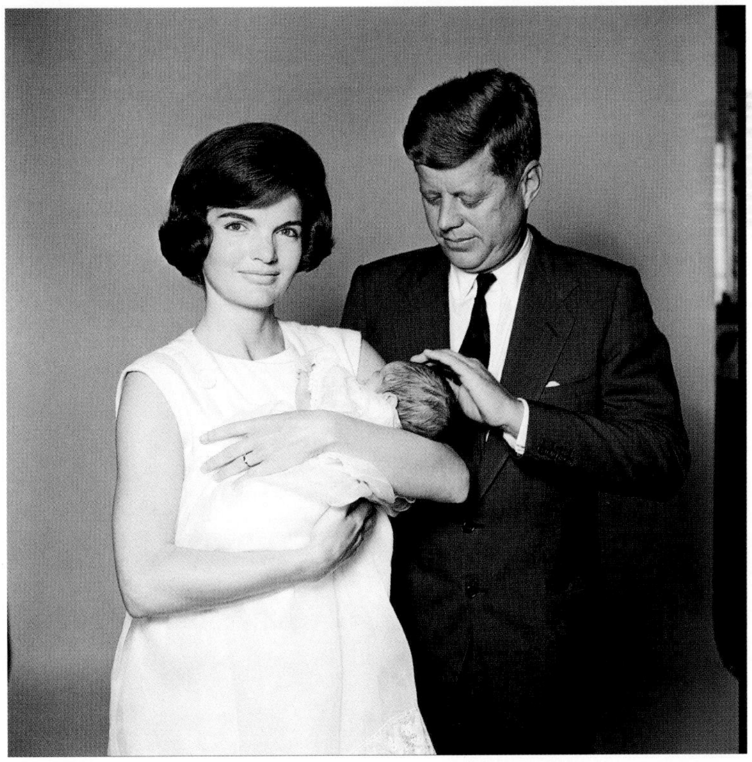

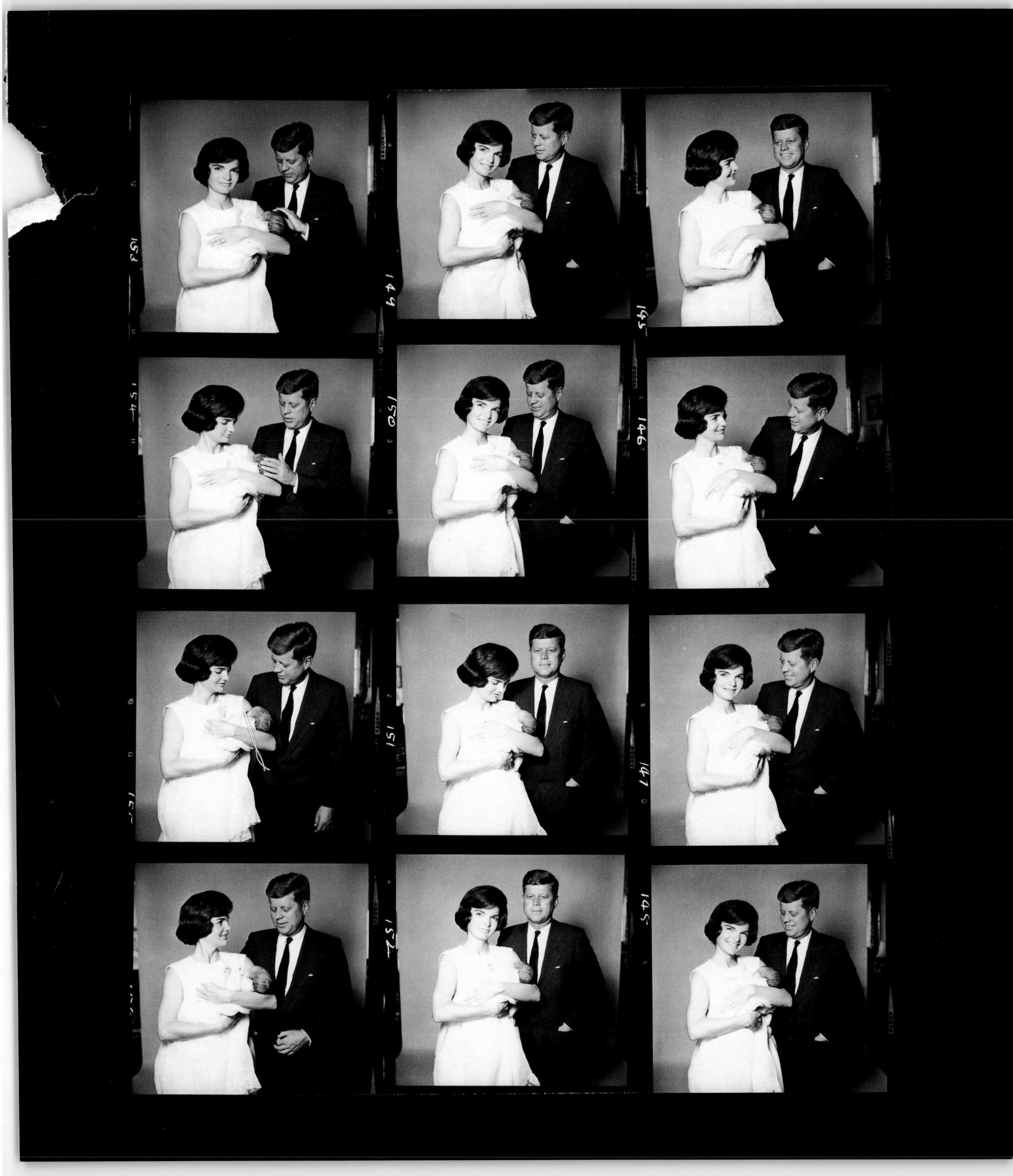

The QUALITY I ADMIRE THE MOST in my husband

is his INTELLECTUAL CURIOSITY—

and that is a quality we both

WISH TO ENCOURAGE IN OUR CHILDREN.

—Jacqueline Kennedy, "Your Child's World," *Times-Herald*, December 11, 1960

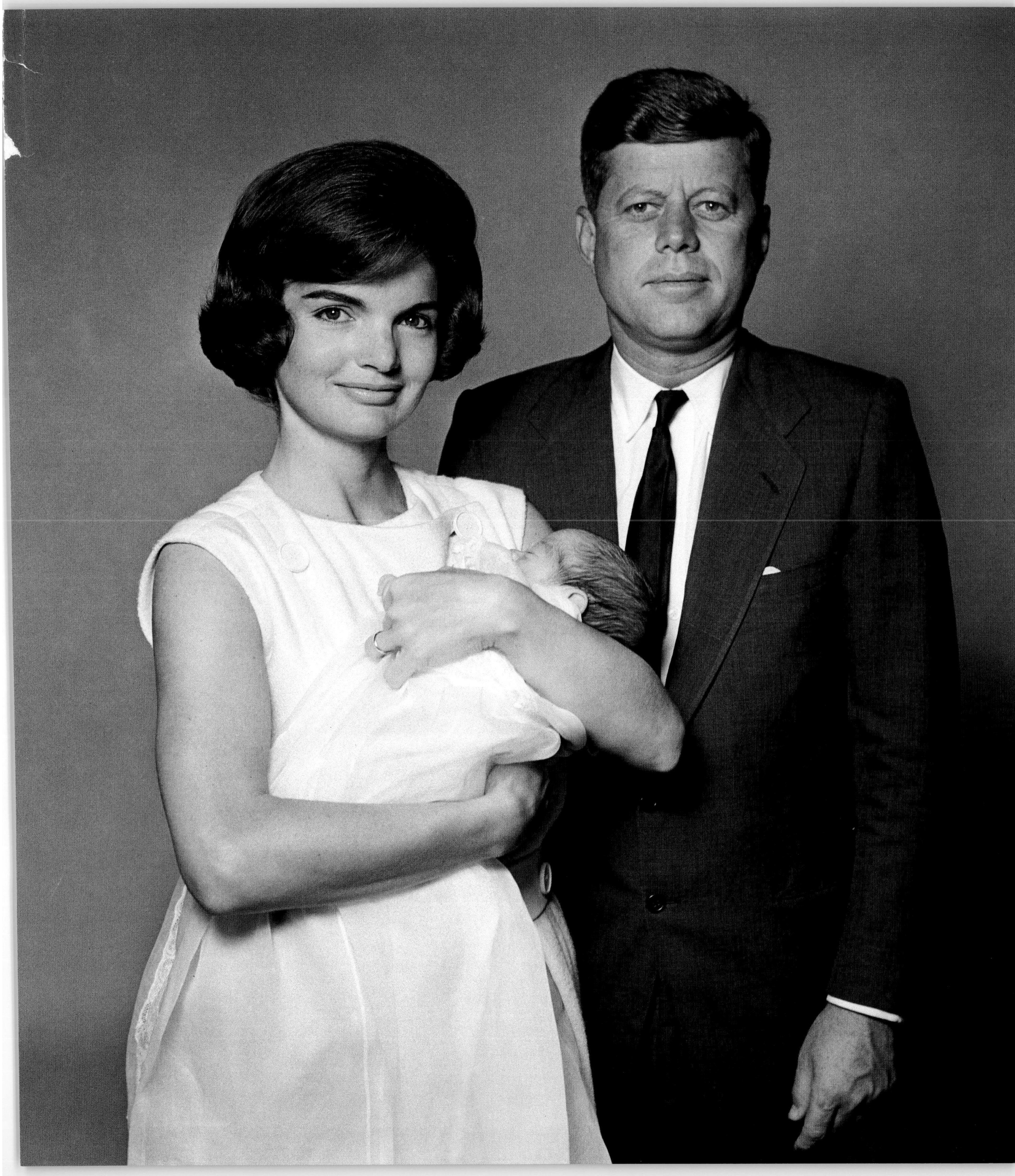

APPENDICES

BIBLIOGRAPHY

BOOKS

Capote, Truman and Richard Avedon.
Observations.
New York: Simon and Schuster Publishers, 1959.

Dallek, Robert.
An Unfinished Life: John F. Kennedy, 1917–1963.
Boston: Little, Brown & Company, 2003.

Grundberg, Andy.
Brodovitch.
New York: Harry N. Abrams Publishers, Inc., 1990.

Kazanjian, Dodie and Calvin Tompkins.
Alex: The Life of Alexander Lieberman.
New York: Alfred A. Knopf, 1993.

Kennedy, Rose Fitzgerald.
Times to Remember.
New York: Doubleday & Company, 1974.

Lubin, David M.
Shooting Kennedy: JFK and the Culture of Images.
Berkeley: University of California Press, 2003.

Perry, Barbara A.
Jacqueline Kennedy: First Lady of the New Frontier.
Lawrence: University of Kansas, 2004.

Rowlands, Penelope.
A Dash of Daring: Carmel Snow and Her Life in Fashion, Art, and Letters.
New York: Atria Books, 2005.

ARTICLES

Avedon, Richard.
"Exiles: The Kennedy Court at the End of the American Century."
The New Yorker, October 4, 1993, pp. 122–161.

Bender, Marilyn.
"'The Woman Who'...Wins High Fashion's Vote Is Jacqueline Kennedy,"
New York Times, July 15, 1960, p. 17.

"Look at the Birdie."
Newsweek, February 6, 1961, p. 55.

Lowe, Jacques.
"A Photographer's Portrait of Jacqueline Kennedy,"
Los Angeles Times, January 8, 1961, sec. C, pp.14, 16.

Quinn, Sally,
"The Face of New York."
Washington Post and Times-Herald, April 9, 1970, sec. PH, p. 7.

Sargeant, Winthrop.
"Profiles: A Woman Entering a Taxi in the Rain."
The New Yorker, November 8, 1958. pp. 49–84.

Spindler, Amy.
"Making the Camera Lie, Digitally and Often,"
New York Times, July 17, 1997, sec. B, p.7.

Tompkins, Calvin.
"The World of Carmel Snow."
The New Yorker, November 7, 1994, pp. 148–158.

ARCHIVES

John F. Kennedy Library
Boston, Massachusetts

John F. Kennedy Library Foundation
Boston, Massachusetts

The Richard Avedon Foundation
New York, New York

Archives of American Art, Smithsonian Institution
New York Regional Office

PHOTOGRAPHY CREDITS

All of the photographs in this book, except those listed below, were donated to the Smithsonian Institution by Richard Avedon, along with all rights. The photographs are part of the Photographic History Collection at the National Museum of American History.

19: Both images courtesy of the John F. Kennedy Library Foundation, John F. Kennedy Library, Boston, Massachusetts. Photographer Karen L. Willis, Photograph Studio, The Metropolitan Museum of Art.

22: *Top:* Library of Congress, Prints and Photographs Division, NYWT&S Collection, LC-USZ62-132830, Washington, D.C. *Bottom:* Bouvier-Kennedy Wedding Portrait by Toni Frissell, September 12, 1953. Library of Congress, Prints and Photographs Division, Toni Frissell Collection, LC-USZCR-4892, Washington, D.C.

24: *Top:* Peabody Archives, Orlando Suero Collection, Baltimore, Maryland. *Bottom:* Verner Reed, 1957. From the Verner Reed Archive at Historic New England. Courtesy Historic New England.

26: Robert Vose, April 20, 1956. Library of Congress, Prints and Photographs Division, *LOOK* Magazine Photograph Collection, LC-L9-56-6620-C, Washington, D.C.

33: Presidential party at the park, 1963. NARA's Central Plains Region (Kansas City), ARC identifier 286011.